CUISINE

**DO NOT REMOVE
CARDS FROM POCKET**

Copyright © 1995 by
King Estate Winery, Inc.

New American Cuisine
Pinot Gris Cookbook

Compiled and edited by
Stephanie Pearl Kimmel
Photography by John Rizzo

Includes index.

Library of Congress
Catalog Card Number
95-80581

ISBN 0-9645500-1-6

10 9 8 7 6 5 4 3 2 1

Printed in Hong Kong

NEW AMERICAN CUISINE

PINOT GRIS COOKBOOK

TABLE OF CONTENTS

New American Cuisine
Pinot Gris Cookbook

INTRODUCTION

We at King Estate are proud to underwrite the production of New American Cuisine. The series evolved from our King Estate Pinot Gris Cookbook which has already led an exciting and successful life of its own. Inspired by the cookbook's outstanding chefs and their exciting recipes, First Daughter Productions and Oregon Public Broadcasting approached us with the idea of underwriting a television cooking series based on the book. We accepted. We had discovered, while working with the superb chefs who contributed to the cookbook, a strong new direction in American cuisine. A movement that rejoices in regional influences and celebrates seasonal ingredients. Hence the title New American Cuisine. We hope the series and this companion book provide great enjoyment.

We feel tremendously grateful that Sarah Kemp accepted our invitation to host New American Cuisine. Sarah is the Publisher of *Decanter* Magazine, the internationally acclaimed wine publication. During her ten years at *Decanter* she has traveled the vineyards of the world and personally launched several *Decanter* guides, including those on the wines and food of America. Sarah has created a new

section in the magazine entitled "Gastronome," a monthly exploration of wine and food, and also has a monthly radio spot on London Broadcast News called the "Decanter Opinion." In 1995 she was the keynote speaker at the World Vinifera Conference in Seattle. In her free time Sarah enjoys cooking, vegetable gardening and fly fishing; her enthusiasm and expertise in both her professional and recreational pursuits lend exuberance and authority to the production.

FOREWARD

*I*n 1992, Decanter Magazine brought out its first guide to the wines of the Pacific Northwest — although we're based in London, we're an international magazine, and the wines of the area had begun to win international acclaim. As the publisher, I felt I had to see the landscape and talk with people to do it justice. That first trip involved driving across Washington State and down deep into Oregon; it was more of a voyage of discovery than I had imagined.

While visiting the wineries of the Northwest, I was thrilled to discover that the Northwest was heaven for a food and wine lover like myself. Vineyards were interspersed with orchards and vegetable plots, in a land where matching food and wine was more than a passing topic of casual conversation, it was a way of life.

The seafood, for one thing, was extraordinary. I may live on an island in an ocean, but I'd never seen anything like the diversity of fish and shellfish. I was amazed that so many different fruits and vegetables came from essentially the same place — everything was "local." The wines, which had drawn me here in the first place, were fascinating, going their own way, cheerfully reflecting the land. In Oregon, two varietals stood out, Pinot Noir and Pinot Gris. Pinot Noir, the grape which is best known for producing red Burgundy, is notoriously difficult to grow. In Oregon however, it has found its second home and international acclaim. Pinot Gris is a recent phenomenon; better known as Pinot Grigio in Italy, it shares one important quality with Pinot Noir — both are excellent wines with food.

In the Spring of 1995, I visited King Estate. Perched on a hill, forty minutes' drive from Eugene, Oregon, surrounded by vineyards, the winery reminded me instantly of Burgundy with its classic architecture of a French chateau. The winery (which specializes in Pinot Noir and Pinot Gris), I was amazed to find, had only been founded in 1992, and the wines were already appearing on some of America's restaurants' best wine lists.

The winery was a reflection of much that I'd been discovering in Oregon: Besides the vineyards, there were orchards and a spectacular organic garden for vegetables, fruit, herbs and flowers, (which made for spectacular meals at the winery!). There was a nursery for grapevines. The winery was ultra-modern, a technological marvel, but ecological principles were respected throughout. And, yes, of course, there was a culinary program, pulling it all together. But above all, I found a band of passionate people who believed in wine and food as part of culture, people who were committed to quality and respected wine and foods place as a civilizing influence in today's hectic commercial world.

It came as no surprise that King Estate would underwrite a television series featuring twenty-two of America's most respected and innovative chefs. Wine for the King Estate, as it is for me, is all about the enduring partnership with food. In a world that seems to speed by far too quickly in a blur of mediocrity, it is reassuring to know that there are people who are dedicated to carefully pursuing excellence, from the land to the table.

PINOT GRIS

*P*inot Gris is the fortunate result of a mutation of the Pinot Noir grape. Its coppery-gray fruit is borne on vines that otherwise appear identical to Pinot Noir. Wine historians believe that this mutation occurred in the Burgundy region of France during the Middle Ages. Writings of the period show that the white wines of Burgundy in the fourteenth century were made from Pinot Gris, which was called by the regional name Fromenteau. The power and influence of the Dukes of Burgundy were at their height during this era and the fame of their white wine, which was recognized for its full-bodied character and delicate aroma, spread beyond the borders of France. Cuttings of the vines were carried into Switzerland and from there spread all over central Europe. Records show that by 1375 vines were already widely planted in Hungary, reputedly taken there by the Emperor Charles IV.

In 1568 an Alsatian baron, Lazare de Schwendi, brought Pinot Gris cuttings back to France after a victorious military campaign fighting the Turks at Tokaj. To celebrate his success the grape was called Tokay d'Alsace. In the late seventeenth century, Fromenteau resurfaced in Burgundian lore when the white wines of Volnay became highly esteemed.

This fashionable wine was pale in color because it spent only a short time on its skins during fermentation. The Volnay of this time was considered a "primeur" wine. Hugh Johnson, in his book *Vintage*, tells us that as late as 1775 this white wine was being described as "the finest, lightest, the first to drink."

In eighteenth century Germany, Johan Ruland, a merchant in the Palatinate, came across a wild vine growing on his property. Upon discovering that the fruit made a delightful wine, he began to propagate the vines, which were called Ruländer in his honor. That "wild" vine was actually Pinot Gris that had been planted there centuries earlier.

Although it is known by many names and is made in many regional styles, Pinot Gris is still very much a part of northern and central European winemaking. In Burgundy, it is now called Pinot Beurot. In Germany it is known as Ruländer or Grauburgunder, and it continues to be widely grown in Hungary and other parts of Eastern Europe. In Italy, the varietal is known as Pinot Grigio. The growers there harvest the grapes early while the acid levels are still high, producing a crisp style of wine with a subdued aroma that Italians—and many other people—favor.

In Switzerland, by contrast, where the wine is known as Malvoisie de Valais, the microclimate is conducive to letting the grapes stay as long as possible on the vines, and the desired style of wine is slightly sweet. In Alsace, Pinot Gris (also known by its old name Tokay d'Alsace) is now considered one of the four noble grapes of that region, along with Riesling, Muscat and Gewürztraminer.

In 1965, David Lett of The Eyrie Vineyards made the first American planting of Pinot Gris, in Oregon. David had become familiar with Pinot Gris when he was in Europe researching the climatic needs of Pinot Noir, and he became convinced that both varieties would produce exceptional wines in the long, cool growing seasons of western Oregon. When David came to Oregon to plant his pioneering vinifera vineyard, he brought along all of the Pinot Gris cuttings he could obtain, which came from only four existing vines in the United States, part of the Variety Collection at the University of California at Davis. His first vintage was 1970, and although he made just enough for enjoying at home, he knew his intuition had been correct.

Through the seventies, David slowly increased his plantings of Pinot Gris through propagation from the original vines. Production was small, about a barrel a year, most of which was traded to salmon fishermen who recognized early what a perfect match Pinot Gris and salmon make. In 1979 he planted the Stonehedge Vineyard in partnership with John Schetky and in that same year grafted all of his Riesling over to Pinot Gris. Between 1981 and 1984 his production grew at a rapid pace. Around the same time, The Eyrie Vineyards Pinot Noir was gaining international recognition, a development that contributed to the Pinot Gris being tried and accepted, and which allowed Oregon Pinot Gris to gain a foothold in the national marketplace.

Other significant producers from Oregon are Dick Ponzi, who released his first Ponzi Pinot Gris in 1983, and David Adelsheim at Adelsheim Vineyard, who followed with his first release in 1984. In the last few years, the number of Pinot Gris producers in Oregon has increased dramatically as they, and a growing audience of wine consumers, have recognized the outstanding qualities of this versatile grape.

When properly grown and vinified, Pinot Gris produces a delicious white wine with a light but complex aroma, a pale, lustrous rose-platinum color, and a rich mouth feel balanced between fruitiness and acidity. Oregon's climate and soil have proven to be ideal for growing Pinot Gris grapes of superb quality. The long growing season with moderate daytime temperatures and cool nights, in concert with well drained, iron-rich, clay-loam soils, produces Pinot Gris with exceptional flavor, intensity and complexity.

At King Estate we have made a long-term, multi-level commitment to this exciting variety. First, we are in the process of planting what will become in terms of clonal selection and rootstock North America'smost diverse Pinot Gris vineyards. We obtainour vines from Lorane Grapevines, the grafting and propagation facility of clonal selections used will contribute to the wine's complexity. Planting on carefully selected rootstock will control the vigor of the vines, resultingin lower crop yields with greater intensity of flavor. At the same time, King Estate is developing long-term relationships with many of Oregon's finest existing Pinot Gris vineyards. The Estate's grower relations program

emphasizes the importance of obtaining the highest possible quality fruit through meticulous pruning, canopy management, fruit thinning and vineyard Maintenance. King Estate will continue to buy Pinot Gris grapes, even after our own vineyards reach full maturity, to insure both complexity and continuityof style.

The interplay of flavors between food and wine creates a harmony that is one of life's great pleasures. We have had the delightful task of experimenting with different recipes to see how they pair with Pinot Gris. Besides the predictable salmon—grilled, poached or baked, as cakes or mousse, any way

you do it, it's fantastic—we have tried other seafood dishes, including apple-smoked trout with horseradish cream, bourride (a Mediterranean fish stew with aïoli) and grilled spot prawns with olive oil infused with rosemary and garlic. Pinot Gris is so luscious and well-balanced that it marries well with lemon, a difficult assignment for most wines. Osso buco, with its traditional lemon, garlic and parsley gremolata garnish, has been greeted with great enthusiasm by all who have tried it. We have also had a lot of success pairing Pinot Gris with simple roast poultry, such as tarragon chicken, and with rabbit, either in a terrine with herbes de Provence or as a braised loin with wild mushrooms, mustard and thyme. Roasted or grilled pork served with fruit salsas, relishes and chutneys has proven an outstanding pairing, as the wine reflects the fruit flavors of the condiments. And, as might be expected, such Alsatian specialties as choucroute and baekoffe are a delight with Pinot Gris. The real surprise is how well the wine stands up even to the spicy flavors of the Caribbean, the Southwest, Asia and India.

As we became more and more convinced of the versatility of Pinot Gris, the idea for a book of recipes to pair with the wine began to take shape. For a couple of reasons we decided to make it a compilation of recipes from some of the best known chefs in America. Outside of the Pacific Northwest very few people are familiar with Pinot Gris, so we felt the book would be a way to introduce restaurant patrons around the country to the wine. Secondly, we suspected that the chefs' recipes would show a wide range of ingredients and cooking traditions and further confirm our belief in Pinot Gris as a superb companion to many styles of food. From New England to Los Angeles, New York to Hawaii, Miami to Seattle and points in between, some spectacular dishes have been created. So browse through the book, buy some Pinot Gris and start cooking. We think you'll be as delighted with the experience as we are.

NEW AMERICAN CUISINE

PINOT GRIS COOKBOOK

ALICE WATERS

CHEZ PANISSE
BERKELEY

❖

Alice Waters was born April 28, 1944, in Chatham, New Jersey. She graduated from the University of California at Berkeley in 1967 with a degree in French cultural studies. She then trained at Montessori School in London, followed by a seminal year travelling in France.

Alice opened Chez Panisse in August 1971, serving a five-course fixed-price menu that changed daily. The set-menu format remains to this day at the heart of her philosophy: to serve the highest quality products according to the season. A network of farmers and ranchers, sought out and encouraged over two decades, assures Chez Panisse a steady supply of pure, fresh and interesting ingredients. An upstairs café at Chez Panisse opened in 1980 and features an à la carte menu, with an open kitchen and a wood-burning pizza oven. In 1984, Café Fanny, a stand-up café serving breakfast and lunch, opened a few miles from the restaurant.

Alice's vision and dedication have made her the most recognized and influential woman chef working in America. Among her many awards are Best Chef in America and Best Restaurant in America from the James Beard Foundation; *The Cook's Magazine* Who's Who in American Cooking; Les Meilleurs Chefs du Monde in *Cuisine et Vins de France*; Restaurant and Business Leadership Award from *Restaurants & Institutions*; and, from the International Women's Forum, The Woman Who Made a Difference Award. Her board affiliations reflect her passions: the Land Institute, the National Committee of Mothers and Others for Pesticide Limits, Advisors for Public Voice on Food Safety and Health, Advisory Board for the University of California, and many more.

Her publications include: *Chez Panisse Menu Cookbook* (1982), *Chez Panisse Pasta, Pizza and Calzone Cookbook* (1984), *Chez Panisse Desserts* (1988), *Chez Panisse Cooking* by Paul Bertolli, with Alice Waters (1988) and the charming *Fanny at Chez Panisse* (1992). A new book, *Chez Panisse Vegetables*, will be published by HarperCollins in spring 1996.

SALMON BAKED ON A FIG LEAF
WITH PINOT GRIS BEURRE BLANC

Serves 4

If you don't have access to fig leaves, you may substitute grape leaves. You won't get the subtle and delicious tropical scent, but you will get an even, moist texture from steaming the fish in the leaves. This technique works admirably with other firm-fleshed fish, such as halibut or sea bass. Fish wrapped in leaves can also be cooked on a grill.

INGREDIENTS
4 large fig leaves
4 5- to 6-ounce salmon filets
4 tablespoons olive oil
Salt and pepper
Pinot Gris Beurre Blanc (recipe follows)

Preheat the oven to 375 degrees.

Wash the fig leaves and put them on your work surface, shiny side up. In a bowl, gently turn the salmon filets with the olive oil, salt and pepper to coat. Put a salmon filet in the middle of each leaf.

Fold the fig leaf over the fish to make a package. Place folded side down on a baking sheet and pour about 1/2 cup water around. Put the baking sheet in the oven for about 10 minutes. Remember, it will

continue to cook a bit after you take it from the oven, so be careful not to overcook.

Place each package in the middle of a dinner plate and open the leaves out. Drizzle with Pinot Gris Beurre Blanc.

PINOT GRIS BEURRE BLANC
1-1/2 tablespoons white wine vinegar
1-1/2 tablespoons Pinot Gris
2 teaspoons shallots, finely minced
1/4 teaspoon salt
Freshly ground white pepper
1 tablespoon unsalted butter for the reduction, plus
    4 ounces chilled unsalted butter, cut into 8 pieces

Combine the vinegar, wine, shallots, salt, pepper and 1 tablespoon butter in a small, heavy, non-reactive saucepan and boil over medium heat until reduced to about 1 tablespoon.

Remove the saucepan from the heat and whisk in a few pieces of the chilled butter until they have melted creamily into the reduction. Return the saucepan to a burner and, over very low heat, add the remaining pieces of butter one at a time, whisking constantly. The sauce should be creamy in texture and pale in color. Season with additional salt, pepper and/or lemon juice. Hold the sauce in a warm spot until serving time.

Alice suggests beginning a summer meal with a salad of green beans and beets dressed with a chervil vinaigrette, serving the salmon with roasted or steamed new potatoes, and ending with a peach or nectarine tart.

Stephan W. Pyle
Star Canyon

STEPHAN PYLES

STAR CANYON
DALLAS

A native of Big Spring, Texas, Stephan Pyles grew up in his parents' Truck Stop Café. Temporarily sidetracked during college, where he earned a degree in music, he still managed to cook in his spare time. A post-graduation trip to France introduced him to such culinary masters as Alain Chapel and Roger Vergé and reaffirmed his passion for cooking. Stephan returned in 1974 to Dallas where he worked diligently in small restaurants, read all the cookbooks he could find, and spent long hours perfecting his technique. In 1980, he was a Chef's Assistant at The Great Chefs of France Cooking School at Robert Mondavi Winery, where he worked closely with Michel Guérard, the Troisgros brothers and Georges Blanc. He spent time in France in 1981 studying pastry with Gaston Lenôtre.

Finally ready in 1983, Stephan opened the Routh Street Café to unanimous critical acclaim. Its more casual spinoff, Baby Routh, followed in 1987. In 1993, he sold his interest in the restaurants to his business partner and began working on a showcase of New Texas Cuisine, Star Canyon, which opened in May of 1994. The menu features carefully selected products indigenous to Texas and Mexico: Texas wild game and poultry, Gulf Coast seafood, Texas cheeses, barbecue, tamales. Star Canyon's interior is accented with rough-cut Texas limestone, a copper and handtooled leather bar, Saltillo tiles and natural bleached woods. The wood-burning ovens, grills and rotisserie in the open kitchen play key roles in the creation of the dishes, as well as enhancing the view from the dining room.

Craig Claiborne called Stephan "an absolute genius in the kitchen" in *The New York Times*, and *Bon Appétit* credits him with "almost single-handedly changing the cooking scene in Texas." The kitchen at Routh Street, under Stephan's direction, won numerous awards, including *Food & Wine's* Top Twenty-Five Restaurants in America; *Restaurants and Institutions'* Ivy Award; Best New Restaurant in America in *GQ; Esquire* and *USA TODAY;* and *Nation's Restaurant News'* Fine Dining Hall of Fame. Stephan was the first Texan named to Who's Who of Cooking in America and was given The James Beard Foundation's award for Best American Chef: Southwest in 1991. He has published a cookbook, *The New Texas Cuisine* (1993), a comprehensive overview and documentation of culinary styles throughout the history of Texas.

Salad of Poached Pears and Arugula with Port Vinaigrette and Cambazola Toasts

Serves 4

Ingredients

2 cups dry white wine

1/2 cup good quality Port

2 whole cloves

1/2 cup granulated sugar

2 ripe pears

1 teaspoon raspberry vinegar

1 shallot

1 clove roasted garlic

6 tablespoons walnut oil

2 tablespoons vegetable oil

Salt and freshly ground pepper to taste

6 cups arugula, washed, destemmed and dried

4 slices French bread, cut on the bias to a length of
    about 2 inches

2 ounces Cambazola cheese

3 tablespoons walnut halves, toasted and
    roughly chopped

In a saucepan just large enough in diameter to hold 4 pear halves, bring the wine and Port to a boil with the cloves and sugar. Meanwhile, peel and core the pears and cut them in half. Add them, cut-side down, to the boiling poaching liquid and reduce the heat to low. Simmer for 10 to 15 minutes, or until tender when pierced with a skewer. Remove the pears with a slotted spoon and set aside.

Preheat the oven to 400 degrees.

Pour off all but 1 cup of the poaching liquid and reduce it over high heat to 2 tablespoons. Place the reduced liquid in a blender or small food processor and add the raspberry vinegar, shallot and garlic. Blend until smooth and add the walnut oil and vegetable oil in a steady drizzle until incorporated. Taste for seasoning.

Spread the Cambazola cheese evenly on the 4 French bread slices and place on a baking sheet. Bake them just long enough to melt the cheese slightly.

Dress the arugula with the vinaigrette and divide between 4 plates. Serve each salad with half a poached pear at the top of the plate (cut into a fan if desired), the Cambazola toast at the bottom and some walnuts sprinkled around.

ROBBIN HAAS

DRAGONS
SAN FRANCISCO

Robbin Haas is proud to say that he is strictly self taught. He considers himself an inventor, always searching for some new ingredient or working to improve a dish already discovered. Since the age of 11, when he found he had a love for cooking and a natural ability in the kitchen, he has pursued his culinary education on his own. Having travelled the United States as a chef, Robbin learned the importance of regional cuisine at some of the most prestigious hotels in the country: the Loew's Anatole in Dallas, the Ocean Grand in Palm Beach and the Turnberry Isle Resort in Florida.

In Florida he began to develop a new cuisine based on the heritage of southeastern America and its excellent indigenous foods. In 1993 Robbin took over as chef/co-owner of BANG, an intimate and elegant restaurant in the bustling South Beach district, Robbin was one of the founders and leading proponents of New World Cuisine. Robbin's work there was enthusiastically hailed by local critics. In the summer of 1994, he was named one of America's Ten Best New Chefs by *Food & Wine* magazine.

Robbin is currently working on several new Asian concepts with Mark Miller of Coyote Café and Red Sage fame. In the belief that Asian cuisine is the style of cooking that will lead us into the 21st century, they opened a trio of Asian diners in the Washington D.C. area in early 1996. Called Raku: An Asian Diner, the resturants feature upscale versions of Asian street food. Dragons, which will open in San Francisco's Ghirardelli Square in the fall of 1996, explores this concept on a grand scale.

His experience in Florida is reflected in the recipe Robbin created for our cookbook, Cashew-Dusted Soft Shell Crab with Sweet and Hot Pepper Relish and Warm Mango Salsa, is a celebration of Caribbean flavors and an outstanding match with Pinot Gris. "The wine's inherent fruitiness," he notes, "along with the background spiciness, complement this dish perfectly"

Cashew-Dusted Soft Shell Crabs with Sweet and Hot Pepper Relish and Warm Mango Salsa

Serves 4 for first course, 2 for main course

The Sweet and Hot Pepper Relish and the Mango Salsa should be prepared first and can be made up to 24 hours in advance.

Ingredients

4 large soft shell crabs, cleaned and cut in half
(Soft shell crabs are available in the spring by special order through seafood markets and specialty food stores. At other times of the year, shelled jumbo shrimp are a delectable substitute. Use 20 shrimp for a generous first course for 4 people.)
2 egg whites
1/4 cup ground toasted cashews
1/2 cup rice flour
2 tablespoons ground mustard seed
2 tablespoons ground sesame seed
1 teaspoon ground coriander seed
1 teaspoon ground star anise
1 teaspoon ground Szechwan peppercorns
1/2 teaspoon kosher salt
4 ounces dark beer
1 pint peanut oil for frying
Sweet and Hot Pepper Relish (recipe follows)
Mango Salsa (recipe follows)

In a stainless steel bowl, whip egg whites until frothy. Add half the cashews and all of the mustard seed, sesame seed, coriander seed, star anise, salt and beer. Mix well. Add half the rice flour, mix and let stand for 10 to 15 minutes.

In a deep, heavy pan heat the peanut oil to 350 degrees. Dip the cut half of each soft shell crab in rice flour, then immerse in cashew batter to coat. Deep fry in peanut oil for about one minute, then drain on paper towels until cool. Just before serving, refry crab for 2 to 3 minutes until hot and crispy.

To assemble and garnish:
Place 1/4 cup Sweet and Hot Pepper Relish in the center of each of 4 10-inch plates. If too much liquid has accumulated, drain first. Place a soft shell crab on top of relish and dust with remaining ground cashews. Using a spoon, drizzle warm Mango Salsa around plate in a decorative fashion. Serve immediately.

Sweet and Hot Pepper Relish

1 teaspoon ground cumin
1/2 teaspoon kosher salt
1 teaspoon freshly ground green peppercorns
1 tablespoon chives, snipped fine
1/4 cup extra virgin olive oil
2 tablespoons sherry vinegar
1/4 cup red bell pepper, finely diced

1/4 cup yellow bell pepper, finely diced

1/4 cup jicama, finely diced

1/4 poblano chile pepper, finely diced

1/4 cup cucumber, seeded and finely diced

1/2 teaspoon thyme leaves, finely chopped

Combine thyme, cumin, salt, peppercorns, chives, olive oil and vinegar and mix well. Combine all of the diced vegetables and toss with the vinegar and oil mixture. Set aside for at least 10 minutes to let flavors blend.

MANGO SALSA

1/2 yellow bell pepper, seeded and finely diced

1/2 red bell pepper, seeded and finely diced

1/4 cup onion, diced

2 teaspoons garlic, finely chopped

1/4 cup pineapple, diced

1 ripe mango, peeled and chopped

2 tablespoons orange juice

2 tablespoons dry vermouth

1/8 teaspoon cinnamon

Dash allspice

1/8 teaspoon Scotch bonnet pepper, finely diced
   (or substitute dash bottled pepper sauce to taste)

2 tablespoons to 1/4 cup dark brown sugar
   (to taste depending on sweetness of fruit)

2 tablespoons sherry vinegar

Kosher salt and freshly ground green
   peppercorns to taste

Put the red and yellow peppers, onion, garlic and pineapple in a heavy-bottomed saucepan and cook covered over low heat until very soft. Add mango and cook over low heat an additional 20-25 minutes until mixture starts to break down and form its own sauce

Remove saucepan cover and add the orange juice, vermouth, cinnamon, allspice and Scotch bonnet pepper. Cook over high heat until reduced by half. Add sherry vinegar and 2 tablespoons brown sugar, turn heat down and simmer for 10 minutes. Taste. If the mixture is too sharp or spicy, add more brown sugar. Remove from heat and let cool. When cool, purée in blender, but do not strain. Refrigerate, covered, until ready to use, then reheat to warm just before serving.

ANNE ROSENZWEIG

ARCADIA
NEW YORK CITy

❖

Chef/owner Anne Rosenzweig of Arcadia came to the restaurant business via anthropology. After graduating from Columbia University, Anne spent several years doing field work in Africa and Nepal. During this time she became interested in food and its preparation, and, on her return to the United States, she gave up anthropology and began her basic training as an unpaid apprentice in several New York restaurants. In 1981, she started working at Vanessa in Greenwich Village as brunch chef, then became pastry chef, and finally head chef. It was at this time that her cooking was singled out by *The New York Times* for its originality and creativity. After leaving Vanessa, she worked as a consultant to several New York restaurants while planning her next venture.

In 1985, Anne opened Arcadia and praise from reviewers and diners came immediately. This fifty-seat restaurant serves dishes Anne calls "innovative American," a style for which she has become well known. She takes proven classics and gives them unexpected twists, creating hearty food with rural roots and urban polish. For her work at Arcadia, she was listed in the Who's Who of Cooking in America and has been featured in countless major food magazines and trade publications. In 1986, she published *The Arcadia Seasonal Mural and Cookbook*, which includes recipes created for the restaurant plus reproductions of the striking Paul Davis murals that adorn it. She is currently working on a new coobook.

In 1987, while still maintaining her role at Arcadia, Anne became part of the team that was brought together to rejuvenate the '21' Club, the New York landmark that began as a Prohibition speakeasy. In 1993, Anne was selected by the White House to serve on the "Kitchen Cabinet," a panel of three chefs that advises the Clintons on American food. In the fall of 1995 she unveiled her most recent project, The Lobster Club, named for the sandwich that is one of Anne's signature dishes. Exuberant reviews for its eclectic and informal menu have already appeared in *The New York Times*, *Travel and Leisure*, and *Condé Nast Traveler.*

Anne is a founding board member of the International Association of Women Chefs and Restaurateurs. She also devotes a great deal of her time to charitable fundraising and teaching across America. We appreciate her generous contribution of three recipes, showcasing quite different ingredients and techniques, that she feels marry well with Pinot Gris.

GRILLED LEEKS IN PUFF PASTRY WITH ONION CONFIT

Serves 4

INGREDIENTS

4 medium onions

2 tablespoons butter

1/2 cup red wine

4 medium leeks

3/4 cup to 2 cups chicken stock

4 tablespoons unsalted butter

Salt and pepper to taste

4 3"x3" baked puff pastry bouchées (homemade or
   purchased)

Beurre Blanc (see recipe on page 22)

2 tablespoons chopped chives

Preheat oven to 375 degrees.

Make onion confit. Thinly slice the onions. Melt butter in a heavy-bottomed casserole. Add onions, cover and sweat them gently until translucent. Uncover and place in the preheated oven. Cook, stirring occasionally, until they are light brown and most of the liquid has evaporated. This will take approximately 1 hour. Add the red wine and continue cooking until all the liquid has evaporated. Stir often to prevent the onions from burning. The confit can now be stored, covered, in the refrigerator for up to two weeks.

Trim bottoms of leeks, keeping the root cap intact. Quarter lengthwise to within 2" of the root. Wash carefully. Place in a shallow pan, dot with butter and add enough stock to come one-quarter of the way up the side of the leeks. Season with salt and pepper. Cover tightly with aluminum foil and cook over medium heat until leeks are tender, about 10 to 15 minutes. The leeks can be cooled and kept in the braising liquid for several hours.

To assemble:

Reheat onion confit, moistening with additional chicken stock if necessary. Briefly grill the leeks on both sides until hot and marked. Center bouchées on plates and remove lids. Fill 3/4 of the way with onion confit. Place root end of a leek in each bouchée and curve the rest onto the plate. Sauce with Beurre Blanc and garnish with chives. Replace the puff pastry lids at a jaunty angle and serve.

SWEET GORGONZOLA AND MASCARPONE FRITTERS

Serves 6

The rich and aromatic qualities of the macadamia nuts and the two cheeses make this a luxurious first course.

INGREDIENTS

1 pound sweet Gorgonzola cheese

4 tablespoons unsalted butter

3/4 cup flour, plus an additional 3/4 cup flour
    for dredging

1/2 cup milk

1/2 cup mascarpone cheese

1 egg yolk

2 tablespoons Dijon mustard

Freshly ground pepper to taste

2 cups macadamia nut pieces, lightly toasted

2/3 cup fresh bread crumbs

2 eggs, lightly beaten

1/4 cup clarified butter

8 cups mixed salad greens

1/4 cup balsalmic vinaigrette made with 1 tablespoon
    balsamic vinegar, 3 tablespoons olive oil, salt and
    pepper to taste

Trim Gorgonzola and cut into small pieces. Melt butter and add 3/4 cup flour, stirring with a whisk. Add milk, stirring rapidly. Add Gorgonzola and mascarpone and blend well. Remove from heat and add egg yolk, mustard and pepper.

Line an 8" square baking pan with parchment paper. Pour in fritter batter and smooth the top. Refrigerate at least 2 hours to firm.

Put macadamia nuts and bread crumbs in a food processor and pulse until chopped fine and well blended.

When ready to serve, unmold cheese mixture and cut into 12 squares. Dredge each square in remaining 3/4 cup flour, dip into beaten eggs, and finally coat with crumb and nut mixture.

Heat clarified butter and sauté fritters until golden brown. Drain on paper towels. Put 2 squares in the center of each plate and surround with salad greens lightly dressed with balsamic vinaigrette.

SMOKED TROUT SALAD WITH ENDIVE AND PEARS

Serves 4

INGREDIENTS

2 smoked trout (approximately 8 ounces each,
   skinned, boned and broken into 1/2″ pieces)

1 head curly endive

1 cup (packed) fresh chervil, finely chopped

2 ripe comice pears, peeled, cored and cut into
   1/3″ slices

VINAIGRETTE

2 tablespoons champagne vinegar

1/4 cup hazelnut oil

1/4 cup light oil (sunflower, olive or the like)

Salt and pepper to taste

Grated zest of 1 lemon

Mix vinaigrette ingredients. Add half the chervil. Dress the endive and pear slices lightly with the vinaigrette and arrange as a bed in the center of a large plate. Using the same bowl, gently toss the smoked trout and remaining chervil together. Artfully strew pieces of trout and chervil over the pears and greens.

CHARLIE TROTTER

CHARLIE TROTTER'S
CHICAGO

◈

Charlie Trotter started cooking in 1982 after graduating with a degree in political science from the University of Wisconsin. At that time, he embarked on an intense four-year period of work, study and travel, including stints with Norman Van Aken, Bradley Ogden and Gordon Sinclair. He lived in Chicago, San Francisco, Florida and Europe, "reading every cookbook I could get my hands on and eating out incessantly."

A year before opening his restaurant, Charlie catered exclusive dinner parties for prominent business and social leaders in Chicago. This permitted him to fine tune his recipe ideas and food and wine combinations. Through this experience he began to shape the concept of his "dream restaurant," which became a reality in August, 1987. Over an 18-month period, he worked closely with the architects and construction crew to ensure that everything was exactly as he wanted. This attention to detail carried over into the design, preparation and presentation of the food, making Charlie Trotter's an instant success with both critics and the public. The restaurant was awarded a Four-Star rating by *Chicago Magazine*.

The ceiling-high wine rack in the entrance bar of the renovated 1908 Lincoln Park West brownstone that houses Charlie Trotter's is a bold testimony to the owner's appreciation of wine. "Wine is as important as the food in the eating-out scenario," he says. The rest of the restaurant is understated; "Our colorful staff and good food are enough to enliven the restaurant," he says.

The following are Charlie's notes on the pairing of Pinot Gris with his foie gras recipe: "This is a wine of unusual richness and intensity for this variety. The elements of smoky bacon, fatty foie gras and buttery greens in the dish enhance this effect. Yet the wine's fruit balance also counters the richness; apple skin, pear and peach tones seem to lighten the intermingled flavors. This Pinot Gris also possesses a streak of exotic spice that matches the curry in the slightly sweet carrot broth, and has a fine acidity to match that of the ramp greens. The wine leaves the palate feeling refreshed rather than clobbered and a lingering warm finish continues the pleasure."

Hudson Valley Foie Gras with Morel Mushrooms, Ramp greens, Smoked Bacon and Curried Carrot Broth

Serves 4

Fresh Hudson Valley Foie Gras is available by special order from specialty butchers or by phone through D'Artagnan (1-800-327-8246). Fresh foie gras from the West Coast can be ordered from Sonoma Foie Gras (707-938-1229).

Ingredients

Curried Carrot Broth (recipe follows)

1/2 pound morels, thoroughly cleaned (substitute portobello mushrooms when morels aren't available)

4 cloves garlic, coarsely chopped

2 sprigs fresh rosemary

2 sprigs parsley

1 tablespoon finely chopped parsley

2 tablespoons beef stock

2 tablespoons butter

2 shallots, finely chopped

4 ounces smoked slab bacon, cubed

2 tablespoons butter

1 pound ramp greens (substitute collard greens, mustard greens or spinach—or a combination)

4 1/2-ounce slices of foie gras

Curried Carrot Broth

2 cups carrot juice

3 tablespoons curry butter (recipe follows)

Place carrot juice in a heavy saucepan and bring to a boil. Reduce heat and simmer until juice is reduced to 1 cup. Strain through cheesecloth, return to pan and set aside.

Make curry butter:

2 teaspoons vegetable oil

1 shallot, chopped

1 small clove garlic, chopped

2 ounces cooking apple, chopped

1/2 teaspoon curry powder

Pinch turmeric

Pinch paprika

1/4 small bay leaf

4 tablespoons unsalted butter

Sweat the shallot and garlic in 1 teaspoon of vegetable oil until translucent. Add the chopped apple and cook over low heat until the apple is soft. Add the curry powder, turmeric, paprika, bay leaf and the other teaspoon of oil and cook over a low flame for 20 minutes, stirring occasionally. Remove bay leaf and purée. Pass through a fine sieve. Cool purée to room temperature. Cut butter into pieces and place in a food processor with the cooled purée and process until smooth. Keep refrigerated until needed. Just before serving bring reduced carrot juice back to a boil and whisk in the curry butter. Season with salt and pepper.

Thoroughly clean morels by soaking in salted water for about 10 minutes, then rinsing under cool running water several times. Drain. Place morels in a roasting pan with the garlic, rosemary, parsley and beef stock. Cover with foil and roast in a 350 degree oven for 20 minutes. Meanwhile, sweat shallots with the butter in a heavy saucepan. When the morels are finished roasting, add them to the shallots and sauté them over medium heat for about three minutes to blend flavors. Season with salt and freshly ground pepper to taste, then sprinkle with the chopped parsley. Set aside, but keep warm.

Place bacon cubes in a heavy skillet and cook over medium high heat until the fat is completely

rendered. Remove bacon and set aside. Add 2 tablespoons butter to the bacon fat in the pan and add the thoroughly washed and dried greens. Sauté over medium heat until wilted. Set aside, but keep warm.

Heat a non-stick heavy skillet over medium heat. Quickly sear the foie gras pieces, approximately 45 seconds on each side. Take care to not overcook or the foie gras will begin to melt. Season with salt and pepper to taste.

To assemble:
Mound one-quarter of the greens into the center of each of four warm flat bowls, such as a rimmed soup plate. Place seared foie gras on top. Arrange morels and bacon about the plate, then pour the Curried Carrot Broth around the dish.

GREG HIGGINS

HIGGINS
PORTLAND, OREGON

*A*s a boy in the farming community of Eden, in upstate New York, Greg Higgins sometimes played hooky from school to spend the day gathering crayfish in local streams or experimenting with recipes he'd discovered in Fanny Farmer. He developed an appreciation of seasonal produce working on truck farms in the summer. At 15, he became an apprentice to a Swiss sausage and cheese maker, an experience that had a strong influence on his style. In college, he worked in the kitchen of an Italian restaurant.

Finishing a degree in fine arts didn't diminish Greg's interest in cooking. He travelled through Europe, then worked at the Sun Valley Lodge and several restaurants in Seattle. In 1984, Higgins signed on as sous chef for the newly renovated Heathman Hotel in Portland. He was promoted to executive chef in 1985, overseeing all of the hotel's food operations and developing its popular Bakery and Brew Pub.

In the spring of 1994, he opened his own restaurant, Higgins, an American brasserie with a constantly evolving menu based on organic and seasonal Oregon ingredients.

Greg collaborated with several other Northwest chefs on the *Pacific Northwest the Beautiful Cookbook* (Collins, 1993) and is one of the driving forces behind the International Pinot Noir Celebration held in Oregon each summer. He is also an enthusiastic cyclist. *Better Homes and Gardens* captured an accurate image of Greg in this quote: "Although Higgins doesn't reel in the fish or pick edible wild berries and mushrooms, he has a network of locals who do. He even keeps a sharp eye out for new people who have something to add to the larder as he pedals along the back roads of the Willamette Valley or through Oregon's wine country."

TERRINE OF RABBIT AND CHICKEN WITH SOUR CHERRIES

Serves 16 as an appetizer

Although this recipe is made over the course of four days, it doesn't require much time in total, and it's simple to make. We were somewhat skeptical about using plastic wrap instead of fatback to line the terrine, but the result was moist, delicious and much lower in fat.

INGREDIENTS

1 pound skinless, boneless chicken breast, cut into
    3/4″ cubes

1 pound boneless rabbit hindquarter, cut into
    3/4″ cubes

1 pound fresh pork shoulder, ground

1 medium onion, cut into 1/2″ slices

2 cups dry white wine

6 bay leaves

Seasoning salt mixture:

    2 heaping tablespoons salt

    1/2 teaspoon ground allspice

    1/2 teaspoon ground coriander

    1/2 teaspoon ground white pepper

1/2 cup bread crumbs

1/2 cup heavy cream

2 tablespoons shallots, minced

1 tablespoon garlic, minced

1/2 cup dried sour cherries (other dried fruit
    may be substituted)

1/2 cup toasted hazelnuts

3 ounces kirschwasser

4 ounces thinly sliced ham

(start this recipe 4 days ahead)

DAY 1:

Mix the chicken, rabbit, onion, bay leaves and wine. Make the seasoning salt by mixing the salt, allspice, coriander and white pepper in a small bowl. Season the chicken and rabbit mixture with two level tablespoons of the seasoning salt mixture, cover with plastic wrap and refrigerate overnight.

DAY 2:

In a large mixing bowl, combine the ground pork with the remaining seasoning salt, kirschwasser, shallots, garlic, cream, bread crumbs, dried cherries and hazelnuts. Mix quickly and thoroughly, taking care not to allow the mixture to warm noticeably. Drain the rabbit and chicken and remove the onions and bay leaves. Add the rabbit and chicken to the pork mixture. Evenly combine the meats. Wrap and refrigerate.

Line a 8″x 4″ x 2-1/2″ loaf pan or pâté mold with plastic wrap, allowing lots of overlap. Line the plastic wrap with thinly sliced ham, overlapping each slice by 1/4″ and extending far enough over the edge of the pan to enclose the top of the filled terrine. Carefully fill the lined pan with the forcemeat mixture, packing it down firmly to avoid air pockets. Mound the mixture in an even slope toward the center, where it should stand at about 1″ above the pan's edge. Enclose with the sliced ham and plastic wrap. Cover with aluminum foil and refrigerate overnight.

DAY 3:
Preheat oven to 375 degrees.
Place the pan in the center of a larger roasting pan and add enough boiling water to come halfway up the side of the pâté pan. Bake for about 1 hour and 15

minutes, or until the terrine is firm and the juices run clear when a skewer is inserted in its center. Remove from the oven and press with a small board and a weight until cooled to room temperature. Refrigerate the terrine overnight.

DAY 4:
Unmold the pâté. Slice and serve with chilled Pinot Gris, a fresh baguette, good mustard and a salad of greens with vinaigrette. The baked terrine will keep refrigerated for 7 to 10 days and can be frozen for up to 2 months.

SUSAN SPICER

BAYONA
NEW ORLEANS

Susan Spicer grew up in a family of seven children with hearty appetites and a mother who was an inspired, and active, cook. The first dish she learned to prepare (other than mustard sandwiches) was crêpes, although they were called "roll-up pancakes with jelly." She reminisces: "My mother taught me so that I could make them for my little brother and myself while we watched *Popeye* at 7 a.m. on Sunday morning." In her high school years she specialized in homemade French fries, huge bowls of fudge ripple ice cream, and Rice-a-Roni. As she puts it, "I've made some progress since then."

Susan began her professional cooking career in 1979 as an apprentice to chef Daniel Bonnot at New Orleans' Louis XVI Restaurant. After a *stage* with chef Roland Durand at the Hotel Sofitel in Paris in 1982, she returned to New Orleans to open, as chef de cuisine, the 60-seat bistro, Savoir Faire, in the St. Charles Hotel. In 1985 she travelled extensively in Europe and California, returning to work at the New Orleans Meridien under the direction of consulting chef Marc Haeberlin of L'Auberge de l'Ill,

the three-star restaurant in Alsace. In 1986, Susan opened the tiny Bistro at Maison deVille in the Hotel deVille in New Orleans. After nearly four years as chef, she formed a partnership with Regina Keever in 1990 and opened Bayona in a beautiful 200-year-old Creole cottage in the French Quarter.

With solid support from local diners and critics, Bayona soon began to earn national attention. Susan was named one of the Ten Best New Chefs by *Food & Wine* in 1989, and Bayona was named one of Top 40 Places to Dine in the United States by *Gault Millau*. She has been featured in numerous publications, including *Gourmet*, *Bon Appétit*, *Food Arts*, *Elle*, and *Travel and Leisure*. She has been a guest chef at the James Beard House and in 1993 was the recipient of the James Beard Award for Best Chef, Southeast Region.

The Alsatian flavors of Susan's Salmon with Choucroute are a natural partner for Pinot Gris. But then so are the tropical flavors of her Scallops with Mango Vinaigrette, a great illustration of the versatility of the wine, and of the chef.

Marinated Scallops with Mango Vinaigrette

Serves 4 as main course, 8 as first course

Ingredients

4 large limes, juice of all and zest of only 1

12 sea scallops, sliced in half horizontally

2 tablespoons mango vinegar (substitute rice wine vinegar if necessary)

1/2 teaspoon ginger, peeled and minced

1/4 teaspoon ground allspice

1/4 teaspoon cayenne pepper

2 tablespoons dry white wine

1 ripe mango, peeled and cut into small, uniform dice

1/2 red bell pepper, cut in small (1/8″) dice

1 small jalapeño, seeded and minced

6 tablespoons olive oil

3 tablespoons cilantro leaves, chopped, plus sprigs for garnish

Salt to taste

2 cups Boston lettuce, shredded

2 scallions, cut in a julienne about 3″ long

1 large ripe avocado, cut into long thin slices

Juice limes, reserving 3 tablespoons juice and the zest for dressing. In a ceramic or stainless steel bowl, toss scallop slices in lime juice and let stand for 30 minutes. In another bowl, whisk together all other ingredients to make vinaigrette. Taste and adjust seasoning. Toss the lettuce, scallions and avocado together gently and divide among four plates; surround them with scallop slices and spoon vinaigrette over all. Garnish with cilantro sprigs.

Salmon with Choucroute

Serves 4

Ingredients

4 tablespoons olive oil

1 onion, finely diced

1 carrot, peeled and julienned

1 medium jar fresh sauerkraut (about 22 ounces),
 rinsed well under cold water, then drained

1/2 cup dry white wine

1/2 cup chicken or fish stock

1/4 teaspoon juniper berries, crushed

1/2 teaspoon fresh thyme leaves

1 bay leaf

1/4 teaspoon cracked black pepper

4 6-ounce pieces salmon filet

1 teaspoon butter

1 cup additional dry white wine (for sauce)

2 tablespoons cider vinegar

4 tablespoons unsalted butter, cut into small pieces

Preheat oven to 350 degrees.

In a sauté pan, heat 2 tablespoons of the olive oil and add onion and carrot slices. Toss and cook over medium heat until just wilted. Stir in sauerkraut, wine and herbs, spices and broth. Bring to a simmer, cook 5 minutes, and remove to a baking pan or casserole. Add the other 2 tablespoons olive oil to sauté pan and sear salmon pieces, serving side down, until light brown. Turn and sear the other side for 30 seconds. Remove salmon and place on top of sauerkraut in casserole. Bake in oven for 5 minutes. Meanwhile, add wine and vinegar to skillet and reduce to 1/4 of original volume; then add butter, piece by piece, whisking until sauce is creamy. Season with salt and pepper and keep warm.

To serve, divide choucroute mixture among 4 dinner plates. Top each with a salmon filet and pour sauce over. Accompany with small new potatoes sprinkled with chopped parsley.

JEAN-GEORGES VONGERICHTEN

VONG
NEW YORK CITY/LONDON

◈

Jean-Georges Vongerichten is considered one of the front runners of multi-cultural cuisine in New York. Born and raised in Alsace, France, Jean-Georges started cooking at the age of 15 as an apprentice under Paul Haeberlin of the Auberge de l'Ill. He then went on to work with Paul Bocuse and, finally, Louis Outhier at L'Oasis in the South of France; all three restaurants have three Michelin stars. With this experience, he participated in opening ten restaurants around the world, including those in the Oriental Hotel in Bangkok, the Meridien in Singapore and the Mandarin Hotel in Hong Kong.

Jean-Georges arrived in New York in 1986, immediately wowing diners and critics as chef at Lafayette in the Drake Swissôtel. While there, he earned a four-star review from *The New York Times*, and helped boost the reputation of the restaurant to one of the best in the city. After this success, he went on to open JoJo, his own Manhattan bistro, which was named *Esquire*'s Best New Restaurant of the Year. In 1994, he was nominated for the James Beard Best American Chef: New York City award, in recognition of his accomplishments at JoJo.

Two years after the phenomenal success of JoJo, Jean-Georges dazzled New Yorkers with his Asian fantasy, Vong, which imaginatively merged the ingredients and seasonings of Thailand with the refinement of classical French technique. In November of 1995 he opened a second Vong in London.

Jean-Georges was a leader in the movement toward the use of vegetable juices, vinaigrettes, broths and flavored oils with their clear colors and bright flavors. The recipe he created for our cookbook— Lobster with Thai Spices—is a symphony of succulence, sweetness and spiciness, with a slight citrus tang from the lemon grass. Jean-Georges and Christophe Michaud, Vong's general manager, feel that "Pinot Gris is a great wine to go with the lobster due to its richness in exotic fruit, but with some nice acidity and the honey and spice tones that you need to support this quite spicy dish."

Lobster with Thai Herbs

Serves 4

Ingredients

4 live lobsters, about 1-1/2 pounds each

1/2 teaspoon yellow curry paste (available in the
    Asian section of supermarkets)

1/2 teaspoon red curry paste

1/2 teaspoon green curry paste

2 teaspoons unsalted butter, plus a little butter for
    warming up the lobster meat

1 piece lemon grass, cut into bâtonnets about
    an inch long

2 lime leaves (available in Asian grocery stores)

1/2 medium carrot, shredded

1 tablespoon turmeric

1 cup white Port, Sauternes, or other similar
    dessert wine

1 golden delicious apple, peeled, cored and cut in
    fine julienne

1/2 cup heavy cream, whipped

1 teaspoon peanut oil

2 medium bok choy, cut in 1/2" pieces

1 tablespoon chopped cilantro leaves

To prepare lobsters:

Put the lobster into a large pot of salted boiling water
and cook for 4 minutes. Plunge into a bowl of ice
water to cool, then drain. Using a cleaver, cut
through the lobster at the point where the head and
tail meet. Separate the legs where they connect to
the body. Using a small sharp knife, cut away any
connective tissue and clean out the inside of the
head leaving the shell intact. Return the cleaned
head to boiling water and blanch for 30 seconds.
Set aside to use as garnish. With a pair of small,
sharp scissors, cut through the center of the
underside of the tail, being careful not to cut into
the meat. Trim down each side of the underside of
the tail. Slipping your hand under the tail meat,
gently release it from the shell, trying to maintain it
in one piece. Remove the intestinal tract. Crack the
claws and carefully remove the meat in the largest
pieces possible. Place in a small bowl, cover tightly
and refrigerate until ready to assemble dish. This
can be done up to 4 hours ahead.

For the sauce base, mix the 3 curry pastes. In a sauté
pan, melt the butter, add the curry mixture and
sweat it for a minute. Add lemon grass, lime leaves,
carrots and turmeric and continue to sweat for a few
minutes. Add white Port and reduce by half. Add
apples and simmer for 3 minutes. Cool and reserve.

Just before serving, heat the sauce base and stir in the whipped cream. Season with salt to taste and keep warm. Cut the lobster into 1/2″ medallions. In a sauté pan, melt a little butter and heat the lobster slowly for about 4 minutes, taking care not to overcook. Sauté the bok choy with the peanut oil until tender. Heat the lobster head in oven for a few minutes.

To assemble:
Arrange bok choy in the center of each plate. Place the head shell on top and fill with lobster meat. Nap with sauce and garnish with a scattering of chopped cilantro.

MICHEL RICHARD

CITRUS
LOS ANGELES

◈

Michel Richard, born in Brittany and raised in Champagne, started his career at age 13 as an apprentice in a small restaurant and pastry shop. At 19, he moved to Paris where he quickly rose to the top position at Gaston Lenôtre's celebrated pâtisserie. In 1974, Michel arrived in Manhattan to serve as executive chef at Lenôtre's first shop in the United States. In 1977, he moved to Los Angeles and opened his own very successful French pastry shop. Ten years later, with the creation of Citrus, Michel Richard realized his lifelong dream: to cook in his own restaurant. As owner and executive chef of Citrus, Michel expresses his seemingly unending creativity.

Michel has received numerous awards. In 1994 he was named one of the Five Best Chefs in America by The James Beard Foundation as well as Chef Restaurateur of the Year by the Chefs in America Foundation. His restaurant has been recognized in *Food & Wine*'s Top Twenty-Five Restaurants in the United States and in *Nation's Restaurant News*' Fine Dining Hall of Fame. He received three toques in *Gault Millau* and the Ivy Award from *Restaurants and Institutions*. Michel was named as the James Beard Foundation's Best American Chef: California in 1992. That same year, he was named a Chevalier in the National Order of Merit by the President of the French Republic for his professional excellence and remarkable success in the United States.

While reflecting Michel's French roots and classical training, Citrus is also very much a California restaurant. Its pale yellow and white wicker create a light, airy ambiance that harmonizes perfectly with the fresh, sunny flavors of the kitchen. The sauces are intensely flavored stock, vegetable and herb reductions. While Michel is not dogmatic, butter and cream are primarily reserved for use in desserts.

The ongoing popularity of Citrus has encouraged Michel and his partners to pursue new opportunities: in 1990, the Broadway Deli in Santa Monica and, in 1991, Citronelle in the Santa Barbara Inn. This successful hotel-restaurant concept led to opening several Latham Hotel restaurants: a Citronelle in Washington D.C. and a Michel's Bistro in Philadelphia. In the summer of 1994, Bistro M opened in San Francisco.

Michel's cookbook, *Michel Richard's Home Cooking with a French Accent*, was published in 1993. He was featured in the *Cooking with Master Chefs* television series hosted by Julia Child and seen on public tevelision.

Mussels with Basil Hollandaise

Serves 4 as a first course

Ingredients

24 mussels

3 sprigs basil, stems only (reserve leaves for
Hollandaise)

1 shallot, chopped

1/4 cup dry white wine

1/2 teaspoon freshly ground black pepper

Basil Hollandaise (recipe to follow)

To prepare the mussels:

Buy mussels that have tightly closed shells. Scrub
the shells with a stiff brush and remove the beards
with a small knife. Place the mussels, basil stems,
shallots, white wine and pepper in a wide pan.
Cover tightly and cook, shaking the pan often until
the mussels open, about 3 minutes. Discard any
mussels that do not open. Remove the mussels
immediately from the pan with a slotted spoon to
prevent overcooking and toughening.

Remove the upper half of each shell and discard.
Detach the mussels, but leave them in the shell.
Place on a baking sheet, cover with plastic wrap and
refrigerate until ready to use.

Preheat broiler. Unwrap the mussels and top each
with a teaspoon of Hollandaise, spreading evenly to
the edges of the shell. Place under broiler until the
Hollandaise begins to brown. Divide the mussels on
4 plates and serve immediately.

Basil Hollandaise

3 sprigs basil, leaves only

5 egg yolks

1 to 2 teaspoons strained lemon juice

1/2 cup olive oil

Salt

Blanch the basil leaves in boiling water for 1 minute.
Drain and plunge immediately into ice water. Drain
on paper towels and squeeze out the excess water.

Place the egg yolks in a blender, add 1 teaspoon of
the lemon juice and the basil leaves and process until
puréed. Place in bowl over a pan of simmering water.
Whisk continuously until thickened. Remove the
bowl from the water and add the olive oil very
slowly, whisking continuously until completely
incorporated. Add salt and lemon juice to taste.

SUSANNA FOO

SUSANNA FOO CHINESE CUISINE
PHILADELPHIA

❖

Susanna Foo was born in Inner Mongolia, China and raised in Taipei, Taiwan. She came to the United States in 1967 and earned an M.A. in library science at the University of Pittsburgh. With absolutely no experience, Susanna and her husband, E-Hsin, joined his family's restaurant business. They opened the second family restaurant, Hu-Nan of Philadelphia, in 1979. In 1987, Susanna and E-Hsin opened their own restaurant, Susanna Foo Chinese Cuisine, to express their own philosophy of cooking.

Susanna Foo learned Hunan cooking from her mother-in-law, Wan-chow Foo; Chinese Northern-style pasta from her cousin, Chao Su; and classic French cuisine from the late Jacob Rosenthal, founder of the Culinary Institute of America. Susanna reinterprets classical Chinese dishes with French techniques. She emphasizes sauces made from reduced stocks, onions, tomatoes and carrots—a major deviation from traditional Chinese cooking. She finishes the sauces with herbs and spices from all over the world: lemon grass, tarragon, basil, sun dried tomato, ancho chile, star anise and go-chi, a Chinese medicinal herb. This creates a lighter, brighter and more colorful version of classic Chinese sauces. Vegetables are Susanna's passion. She incorporates such non-Chinese greens as endive, radicchio, arugula and mâche into her cooking, and she creates new dishes from such traditional Chinese vegetables and fruits as fresh water chestnuts, baby chrysanthemum, shiitake mushrooms, litchi nuts and Asian pears.

Susanna's honors and awards include being named one of America's Best New Chefs by *Food & Wine* magazine in 1989, Best Chinese Restaurant in the United States by *Esquire*, The James Beard Foundation nominee for Best American Chef: Mid Atlantic in 1992, and Best Chinese Cook in the Country by *Eating Well* magazine in 1992. Her first cookbook, *Susanna Foo Chinese Cuisine: The Fabulous Flavors and Innovative Recipes of North America's Finest Chinese Cook*, was published in late 1995.

Susanna's contribution to our cookbook is a recipe that she learned from her mother-in-law. In China, she made the dish with free-range chicken, various wild mushrooms gathered from the forest and young bamboo shoots. Her adaptation of this classic is a dish with subtle nuances—a little spicy, somewhat hot and with a flavor both sweet and sour. Susanna says: "The fresh and crispy tastes of the Pinot Gris complement well the complexity and slight spiciness of the food. The acidity of the wine stands well with the balsamic vinegar in the sauce. I hope you will enjoy this dish as much as I enjoy your wine." We do.

TUNG AN PHEASANT WITH ARTICHOKE HEARTS AND WILD MUSHROOMS

Serves 4 to 6 as a first course or 2 as a main course

If pheasants are not available, this dish can be made with chicken, preferably free range. To adapt the recipe to chicken, increase the poaching time to 25 minutes. Made with chicken, the recipe will serve 4 as a main course.

INGREDIENTS

2 quarts chicken stock

2 young pheasants, each about 1 pound, cleaned,
   washed, patted dry

3 tablespoons sake or vodka

3 tablespoons soy sauce

1/2 pound chanterelle or shiitake mushrooms,
   thinly sliced

2 cooked artichoke hearts, thinly sliced

1 teaspoon cornstarch

3 tablespoons oil, corn or soybean

1 tablespoon balsamic vinegar

1/4 cup fresh ginger, thinly sliced

1/2 tablespoon sugar

3 cloves garlic, thinly sliced

1 teaspoon salt

1 jalapeño pepper, cored, seeded and chopped or
   2 dried chile peppers, soaked in water for
   20 minutes, then chopped

1 small red bell pepper, thinly sliced

2 scallions, sliced diagonally

2 cups watercress leaves

In a Dutch oven or large soup pot bring chicken stock to a gentle simmer. Add pheasants, cover and poach over low heat for 5 minutes. Do not let liquid come to a boil. Remove pheasants from stock and allow to cool. Reserve cooking liquid. When the birds are cool, remove and discard skin. Carefully cut meat from the bones, working with the grain, then slice into 1/2-inch strips.

Place pheasant meat in a bowl. Combine sake and soy sauce. Mix well and pour over pheasant, allowing meat to marinate while you proceed with the recipe.

Heat oil in a small non-stick skillet. Add mushrooms and cook, stirring for 3 minutes. Mushrooms should not be cooked through. Spoon mushrooms into a bowl. Deglaze pan with balsamic vinegar and add to mushrooms in bowl, along with the artichoke hearts. Reserve. Combine 1/2 cup of the reserved chicken stock with the cornstarch. Mix thoroughly and reserve.

Heat 3 tablespoons oil in a large non-stick skillet. Add ginger, garlic, jalapeño and the pheasant with its marinade. Cook, stirring for 4 minutes. Add the stock-cornstarch mixture to skillet and mix. Add mushroom-artichoke heart combination and cook, stirring, for 4 minutes. Add red bell pepper and scallions and cook for an additional minute. Remove from heat and keep warm.

Blanch watercress leaves for 30 seconds in remaining reserved chicken broth. Strain, then place watercress leaves on four dinner plates (the leftover broth makes a very flavorful soup base). Spoon pheasant mixture over watercress and serve with sweet rice.

DICK CINGOLANI

CAFÉ ARUGULA & ARUGULA GRILL
LIGHTHOUSE POINT & WEST PALM BEACH

◈

*D*ick Cingolani was brought up in the Cape Cod area in a large, first generation Italian-American family. Both of his parents were accomplished cooks and his happiest times were in the kitchen with them, watching, tasting and learning. At an early age he learned to appreciate the flavors of ingredients fresh from their garden, of wild mushrooms from the nearby woods and of the lobsters and clams washed ashore by big Nor'easters. Although cooking was close to his heart, when he moved to Fort Lauderdale in 1963, it was to pursue a successful career in advertising. Almost 20 years later, he realized his dream of turning his avocation into his vocation.

In 1984, Dick and his wife Carolann opened Cingolani's Cucina, a classic Italian restaurant. Their second restaurant, Café Arugula, opened in 1988, featuring a more eclectic menu, showcasing the flavors of New Orleans and the Southwest as well as those of the Mediterranean. These "Cuisines of the Sun," as he called them, met with great and immediate success. His newest restaurant, the Arugula Grill in West Palm Beach, offers a Mediterranean menu with accents from the Orient and the American Southwest.

Although he had no formal culinary education, Dick shares his passion for good cooking by giving classes both at Café Arugula and on television. He is a tireless supporter of community organizations, serving on the board of the American Institute of Wine and Food (AIWF) and chairing the SOS "Taste of the Nation" event in the Fort Lauderdale area. Café Arugula was given a top ranking in the *Zagat, Access,* and *Gault Millau* guides and *Holiday* magazine. It received the prestigious DiRoNa award for 1995.

The recipe Dick Cingolani has created to pair with our Pinot Gris uses the wonderful shrimp of the Florida coast combined with flavors from his Italian upbringing.

FETTUCCINE WITH SHRIMP, ROSEMARY, TOMATO, LEMON AND GARLIC

Serves 4

INGREDIENTS

24 large shrimp

1/4 cup flour

3 tablespoons butter

4 tablespoons olive oil

4 tablespoons garlic, chopped

3 tablespoons fresh rosemary, chopped

1-1/2 cups dry white wine

1 teaspoon lemon juice

2 cups tomato, peeled, seeded and chopped

4 tablespoons Italian parsley, chopped

2 tablespoons capers

Salt and freshly ground pepper to taste

1 pound fresh fettuccine, cooked *al dente*

1 tablespoon lemon zest finely chopped

Shell and devein shrimp, leaving tail shell on. Dust shrimp in flour and sauté in butter and 2 tablespoons of oil over medium heat until just pink, 1 or 2 minutes. Add garlic and 2 tablespoons rosemary and cook for 1 more minute, taking care not to brown garlic. Remove shrimp from pan. Turn heat to high, add white wine, lemon juice, tomatoes, parsley and capers and reduce liquid by half. Return shrimp to pan until just heated through. Season to taste and serve over fettuccine. Garnish with a gremolata made with the lemon zest and the remaining tablespoon chopped rosemary.

Cindy Pawlcyn

Real Restaurants: Mustards Grill, Fog City Diner, Tra Vigne, Bix, Bistro Rôti and Buckeye Roadhouse
San Francisco and The Napa Valley

Cindy Pawlcyn, executive chef and owner of six California restaurants, has been working in professional kitchens since she was 13 years old. Food was an important part of growing up in the Pawlcyn household. Her father's Russian heritage and her mother's Norwegian and German roots were reflected in the great variety of ingredients used in their family meals. As Cindy's interest and aptitude for cooking developed, her mother encouraged her by finding suitable classes for her to attend. By the time she was in high school, she was working five nights a week for a local kitchen equipment company and taking cooking classes. Cindy graduated from the University of Wisconsin-Stout, receiving a degree with honors from the hotel and restaurant administration program. She then worked as a sous chef at the Pump Room in Chicago, where she met her future partners in Real Restaurants, Bill Higgins and Bill Upson.

The trio opened Mustards Grill in the Napa Valley in 1983 with the goal of "redefining and enhancing our native cuisine and giving it the presence it rightfully deserves." The success of Mustards led to a more ambitious concept, the Fog City Diner in San Francisco, a smash hit from the moment the doors opened in 1985. Tra Vigne, BIX, Bistro Rôti and the Buckeye Roadhouse followed, each with its own personality. In 1994, Real Restaurants opened the Buckhead Roadhouse in Chattanooga, Tennessee; Ajax Tavern in Aspen, Colorado; Caffé Museo in the San Francisco Museum of Modern Art and a Fog City Diner in Dallas. In early 1996, a Fog City Diner opened in Las Vegas.

In 1985 Cindy was named one of America's Top Twenty-Five Chefs by *Food & Wine*, and in 1988, she was inducted into the Who's Who of Cooking in America. She has been featured in *Bon Appétit, Rolling Stone* and *Gourmet* as well as in cookbooks by Irene Chambers, Martha Stewart and James McNair. Her own cookbook, *The Fog City Diner Cookbook*, was published in 1993, and a Mustards Grill cookbook is in the works.

Calamari with Ginger and Herb Butter

Serves 4 as an appetizer

Ingredients

1/2 teaspoon salt

Pinch fresh ground pepper

Pinch cayenne pepper

1/4 cup cornmeal

1/4 cup flour

2 cups peanut oil

1 pound calamari, cleaned

1/4 cup buttermilk

6 to 8 tablespoons unsalted butter

1 tablespoon peeled and grated fresh ginger

1 tablespoon peeled and minced garlic

2 tablespoons minced Italian parsley

1 tablespoon minced basil

2 tablespoons minced chives

Heat oil to 375 degrees.

Skin the calamari and rinse under running water. Drain well, then slice into rings.

Mix the salt, pepper, cayenne, cornmeal and flour until thoroughly combined. Dip the calamari into the buttermilk and then toss with the cornmeal and flour mixture to coat. Make sure it is coated evenly. Lower into the hot fat. Cook 3 to 5 minutes, or until golden brown and crispy. Drain on paper towels. Meanwhile melt the butter and, when it becomes frothy, add the ginger, garlic and herbs and swirl to combine. Season to taste with salt and pepper. Pour the butter sauce over the calamari and garnish with a wedge of lemon.

The calamari can be pan fried in a small amount of oil rather than deep fried if you prefer. This recipe is also delectable when made with shelled jumbo shrimp or whole soft shell crabs.

MARK MILLER

RED SAGE
WASHINGTON D.C.

❖

Born and raised in Boston, Mark Miller was drawn to the West Coast to study Chinese art history and anthropology at the University of California at Berkeley. After a period of postgraduate work, Mark made a break from academia to pursue his fervor for cooking, working with Alice Waters at Chez Panisse. In 1979, he left Chez Panisse to open his own restaurant, Fourth Street Grill, where he was free to cook spicier, more rustic food inspired by his travels through Central America, North Africa, Southeast Asia and the Southwest. In 1980, Mark opened his second Berkeley restaurant, the Santa Fe Bar and Grill. There he played a major role in establishing Southwestern food as a nationally recognized and popular cuisine.

In 1984, Mark sold both Berkeley restaurants and moved to Santa Fe, New Mexico to further develop his ideas at the source. He opened the Coyote Café there in 1987. Red Sage, decorated in the sizzling colors and iconography of the American West, opened in Washington D.C. in 1992, and includes a 150-seat restaurant, a 100-seat Chili Bar, three private dining rooms, an in-house bakery and a retail store. In December 1993, he opened a second Coyote Café in Las Vegas, at the MGM Grand Hotel, the largest hotel in the world. A third Coyote Café is in Austin, Texas. His achievements have consistently drawn acclaim in the national press, including *The New York Times*, *The Los Angeles Times*, *Time*, *Metropolitan Home*, *Vogue*, *Bon Appétit* and many others. In 1991, Mark was inducted into the *Nation's Restaurant News* Fine Dining Hall of Fame. Red Sage was named *Esquire's* 1992 *Restaurant of the Year*. Mark's expressive and robust style of cooking is evident in his cookbooks: *Coyote Café* 1989), *The Great Chile Book* (1991), *Coyote's Pantry* (1993), *The Great Salsa Book* (1994) and *Mark Miller's Indian Market Cookbook* (1995). A Red Sage cookbook is also in the works.

Miller will carry his innovative approach into the realm of modern Asian cuisine as he develops his latest projects. Raku: An Asian Diner, serving upscale pan-Asian cuisine based on the street foods of Japan, China, Thailand and Korea, opened in Washington D.C. in December, 1995. Two additional units in the Washington D.C. area opened in spring of 1996. Plans are moving forward for an Asian bistro in San Francisco, which will open late in 1996 at Ghiradelli Square.

PIÑON-CRUSTED PACIFIC SALMON ON FRESH MORELS AND GRILLED FENNEL, WITH GUAJILLO ORANGE-GRAPEFRUIT SAUCE

Serves 4

INGREDIENTS

Guajillo Orange-Grapefruit Sauce (recipe follows)

3 fennel bulbs

1 yellow onion

Olive oil for coating fennel and onions for grilling

1/2 pound fresh morel mushrooms (substitute other wild mushrooms in season)

1/4 cup unsalted butter

2 tablespoons olive oil

2 tablespoons fennel leaves, chopped medium

1/2 cup dry white wine

Salt and freshly cracked black pepper

4 6-ounce salmon filets

1 egg, beaten, to coat top of salmon

1/2 cup pine nuts (toasted and chopped medium-fine by hand)

GUAJILLO ORANGE-GRAPEFRUIT SAUCE

2 cups orange juice

1 cup grapefruit juice

1/4 cup dry white wine

1 cup fish stock (or clam juice)

3 whole guajillo chiles, roughly chopped (available at Latin American markets)

2 tablespoons unsalted butter

Honey to taste (if needed)

To prepare sauce:

Reduce orange juice, grapefruit juice and wine to simple syrup consistency (about 3/4 cup); this will take 30 to 40 minutes. Add guajillo chiles and fish stock or clam juice. Let simmer for 20 minutes or until sauce coats the back of a spoon. Strain and keep warm. Just before serving, stir in butter and serve immediately. If sauce seems bitter, add a touch of honey.

While the sauce is reducing, cut fennel bulb into quarters and slice onion into rings. Toss fennel and onions in a small amount of olive oil, salt and pepper. Cook over medium hot grill until they are just soft, taking care not to burn the onions. The fennel will take a little longer than the onion rings to soften. Set aside to cool. When fennel is cool, cut into smaller pieces. In a 12" non-stick sauté pan, brown 1/4 cup butter and 2 tablespoons olive oil. Add morels (if morels are very large, cut in half) and sauté for 3 minutes, stirring constantly. Add white wine and deglaze pan, reducing liquid until it is almost gone. Add onions, fennel, 1 tablespoon of the fennel leaves, salt and pepper. Sauté for 1 more minute to combine flavors. Adjust seasoning.

Preheat oven to 350 degrees.

Lightly salt salmon filets and sear in hot oil, about 45 seconds on each side. Let cool on rack. Brush salmon tops with beaten egg and pat on a layer of chopped pine nuts. Finish in the oven for 8 to 10 minutes, depending on the thickness of the filets. Be careful not to overcook.

To assemble dish, spoon mushroom-fennel mixture into the center of the plate and place salmon on top. Drizzle the sauce around the edges of the plate and garnish salmon with the remaining fennel leaves.

ROY YAMAGUCHI

ROY'S RESTAURANTS
HONOLULU, MAUI, KAUAI, TOKYO, GUAM, HONG KONG, THE PHILIPPINES AND PEBBLE BEACH, CALIFORNIA

Roy Yamaguchi was born in Japan in 1956. His mother came from Okinawa and his father was a career military man originally from Maui. Brought up in Tokyo until the age of 17, he absorbed much of the Japanese culture. Yet he still vividly recalls visits to Maui to see his grandparents and his first experiences of the Pacific. "My father would drive for hours and hours just to get fresh fish, crabs, octopus and lobster from the piers. It seems that I have always loved to cook, whether it was Portuguese sausage and eggs for breakfast, or a full-on Thanksgiving dinner." Immediately after high school Roy went to the Culinary Institute of America where he received his earliest classical training. After graduating in 1976, he apprenticed in Southern California at L'Escoffier and under the late master chef Jean Bertranou at L'Ermitage. In 1984, he opened a restaurant of his own in Hollywood called 385 North. His highly personal style blossomed there and earned him a feature in *Bon Appétit* in June of 1988 and the honor of being chosen California Chef of the Year by the California Restaurant Writers Association.

At the same time, he knew he wanted to return to Hawaii, so he closed his restaurant, uprooted his young family and moved to Honolulu. The opening of Roy's Restaurant in December of 1988 did not go unnoticed. Within months it was dubbed "the crown jewel of Honolulu's East-West Eateries" by *Food & Wine*, was selected twice by Mimi Sheraton in *Condé Nast Traveler* as one of the Top 50 American Restaurants, named one of *GaultMillau*'s Top 40 American Restaurants; by early 1992 it found itself enshrined in *Nation's Restaurant News'* Fine Dining Hall of Fame. In 1993, Roy was chosen by The James Beard Foundation as Best American Chef: Pacific Northwest.

Roy Yamaguchi has been pivotal in creating a contemporary Hawaiian cuisine and is universally heralded as the leader of the school. Despite this, he still clings to his original conception of his cooking style, which he prefers to call "Euro-Asian." It is, in fact, a highly personal approach, reflecting his heritage, his training and his experience. Roy's contribution to the cookbook, which he selected in concert with his business partner and prize-winning sommelier Randal Caparoso, is a superb choice. The spicy succulence of the sausages, the sweet tones of the yams and curry, and the fresh, almost citrus flavors of the lettuces work brilliantly with Pinot Gris.

Island Style Chicken Sausage with Roasted Yams, Farm Greens and Thai Curry Sauce

Serves 4

Ingredients

Island Style Chicken Sausage

4 ounces boneless dark chicken meat

4 ounces pork fat

4 ounces pork butt

12 ounces boneless white chicken meat, finely diced

2 tablespoons olive oil

1/2 cup onion, finely diced

1/2 teaspoon garlic, minced

1/4 cup red bell pepper, finely diced

1/4 teaspoon fresh ginger, minced

1/2 teaspoon cumin, ground

1/2 teaspoon coriander, ground

1/2 teaspoon cayenne

1/4 teaspoon fresh basil, minced

1/4 teaspoon fresh thyme leaves, minced

2 tablespoons Jamaican jerk sauce (several brands
are usually available in specialty food stores)

12 sausage casings (about 5 feet of hog casing,
rinsed with cold water)

In a mixing bowl, combine the dark chicken meat, pork fat and pork butt. Run through a meat grinder twice. Add the diced white chicken meat and set aside.

Heat the olive oil in a skillet and sauté the onion, garlic, bell pepper and ginger over medium-high heat for 30 seconds. Add the cumin, coriander, and cayenne. Stir and cook for 30 seconds longer. Add to the chicken mixture, then add the basil, thyme and jerk sauce. Mix together thoroughly, then allow to cool. Fill the rinsed casings with the sausage mixture, making links about 3 inches in length. Set aside, covered and refrigerated (formed sausages can be held, well wrapped, for up to 2 days in the refrigerator). About 20 minutes before serving time, poach the links in a skillet filled with barely simmering water for 6 or 7 minutes until they firm up. Drain, then sauté slowly until nicely browned. Alternatively, the sausage may be formed into patties and browned.

Mashed Roasted Yams

1 pound yams

2 tablespoons butter

Heavy cream

Salt and pepper

Wrap yams in heavy foil and roast in a 400 degree oven until fork tender, about an hour. Protecting your hand with a dishtowel, peel yams and place them in a medium bowl. Mash yams, beating in butter and a little heavy cream until smooth. Season to taste with salt and freshly ground black pepper. Set aside, covered, in a warm place.

THAI CURRY SAUCE

2 cups coconut milk

1 tablespoon fresh lemon grass, chopped

2 tablespoons palm sugar (or substitute coconut sugar, both available at Asian markets)

1 large leaf fresh basil

1 teaspoon fish sauce (can be found in the Asian section of most markets)

1 teaspoon garlic, minced

1 tablespoon fresh ginger, chopped

2 teaspoons Thai curry paste (Matsaman brand)

Combine the coconut milk, lemon grass, palm sugar, basil, fish sauce, garlic and ginger in a saucepan with a heavy bottom. Simmer until the sauce reaches the consistency of half-and-half. Add the curry paste and simmer for 5 minutes longer or until the sauce is syrupy. Strain and keep warm.

FARM GREENS

4 ounces of your favorite blend of baby greens

1 teaspoon extra virgin olive oil

Sea salt to taste

Toss together just before assembly.

To assemble:

Place a dollop of mashed yams in the center of large plate. Arrange browned sausage on top of the potatoes. Pour sauce around, then garnish with the dressed greens.

KEVIN MCCARTHY & EVE MONTELLA

ARMADILLO CAFÉ
DAVIE, FLORIDA

Kevin McCarthy and Eve Montella are co-owners and co-chefs at the Armadillo Café in south Florida. Kevin is a 1975 graduate of the Culinary Institute of America and a veteran of ten years with the Gilbert/Robinson Restaurant Company. His job with Gilbert/Robinson involved travelling around the United States opening specialty restaurants. It was during a stint in Dallas that his love for that region's food blossomed. Moving to Miami in 1986, Kevin was the chef at Max's Place before opening the Armadillo Café in 1988.

Eve Montella graduated from the Restaurant School at Florida International University in 1979. Her interest in cooking had been nurtured in her mother's kitchen from early childhood. Eve directed a cooking school and had her own catering company prior to joining forces with Kevin to open the Armadillo Café.

Armadillo Café is a mélange of the culinary influences of south Florida and the American Southwest. Current favorite ingredients include chipotle chiles, sun-dried tomatoes, gold tequila, Hayden mangoes, yellow beefsteak tomatoes, Texas antelope, portobello mushrooms and all of the great Florida seafood.

Among the awards the pair has earned are top ratings in the *GaultMillau* and *Zagat* guides, and the *Miami Herald*. The restaurant was named Tasters Guild Restaurant of the Year in 1992 and was given the *Wine Spectator's* Award of Excellence in 1992, 1993, 1994 and 1995.

Rock Salt Shrimp with Ancho Beurre Blanc and Tomato Tequila Salsa

Serves 4 as first course

To serve as a main course, double the number of shrimp and accompany with seasoned rice or mashed potatoes to soak up the wonderful sauce.

Ingredients

16 jumbo shrimp, peeled and deveined, leaving
    tail on (save the shells)
Shrimp stock (recipe follows)
Ancho Beurre Blanc (recipe follows)
Tomato Tequila Salsa (recipe follows)
1 box rock salt

Hold the cleaned shrimp in a stainless steel bowl until ready to bake.

Shrimp Stock

Reserved shrimp shells
2 tablespoons unsalted butter
1/4 cup chopped shallots
5 or 6 medium cloves garlic, finely chopped
1 cup dry white wine

Heat butter in a large sauté pan, then add the shallots, garlic and the reserved shrimp shells.

Sauté until the shallots and garlic are soft and the shells are pink. Transfer to a large saucepan. Set the sauté pan aside for further use—don't wash it. Cover the shells with the wine and water, set over medium high heat and simmer until the mixture reduces to about 1 cup. Strain and set aside.

Ancho Beurre Blanc

6 ancho chiles, toasted and reconstituted in warm
    water, then cut into strips
2 tablespoons unsalted butter
1/2 cup shallots, finely chopped
1 bunch chives, finely chopped
1/2 cup mushrooms, finely chopped
1/2 to 3/4 cup reserved shrimp stock
1 cup dry white wine
1/4 cup Sauternes (Muscat de Frontignan, Beaumes
    de Venise, Barsac or other similar dessert wine
    may be substituted)
Juice of 2 limes
3/4 cup heavy cream
4 ounces cold unsalted butter, cut into small pieces
Salt
Freshly ground black pepper

Melt the butter in a large sauté pan. Sauté shallots, mushrooms, chives and ancho strips until soft and glazed. Add stock, white wine and Sauternes and reduce to about half the volume. Add lime juice and cream. Reduce again to half the volume. Strain this mixture and press well to extract all the liquid. Return strained sauce to pan and reheat to a simmer. Reduce until sauce is slightly thicker, then begin to whisk in the butter one piece at a time. Add butter until the sauce is sufficiently enriched to your taste. Season with salt and pepper. Hold the sauce in a warm place near the oven or stove, but not on direct heat.

Tomato Tequila Salsa

2 medium sized ripe red tomatoes, peeled, seeded
    and diced medium
1/2 small red onion, finely diced
1 tablespoon cilantro leaves, finely chopped
3 jalapeño peppers, finely diced
Juice of 1 lime
Salt to taste
2 tablespoons extra virgin olive oil
2 ounces gold tequila

Combine all salsa ingredients except tequila in a small bowl. Taste for seasoning. Reheat the sauté pan previously used for the shrimp shells. When the pan is hot, add the tequila and reduce until all the alcohol has burned off and the liquid is almost a glaze. Quickly add the tomato salsa, stir and remove from heat. Retaste the salsa for seasoning. Set aside in a warm place until you are ready to plate the shrimp.

Preheat oven to 400 degrees.

Fill a metal baking pan with rock salt to a depth of about an inch. Place the pan in the oven to heat while you prepare the sauces.

Lightly coat the shrimp in olive oil. Remove the pan of rock salt from oven (the salt should be sizzling hot). Place shrimp directly on hot rock salt and put the pan back in the oven. The shrimp will cook extremely fast with this method. Be prepared to turn the shrimp with tongs in about 2 minutes; shrimp should cook in 5 minutes or less. Serve immediately with the ancho beurre blanc and tomato salsa for garnish.

YELLOWTAIL SNAPPER WITH OYSTER MUSHROOMS, GINGER AND ROASTED PEPPERS

Serves 4

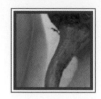

INGREDIENTS

4 6- to 7-ounce portions skinless yellowtail snapper
filet (red snapper or sea bass may be substituted)

Seasoned flour made with 1 cup flour,
1/2 teaspoon salt, 1/2 teaspoon cayenne pepper,
1 teaspoon ground cumin, 1 teaspoon chile
powder and several grinds of black pepper

Egg wash made by whisking together 1 egg,
1 teaspoon Dijon mustard and 1/2 cup milk

1/2 to 1 cup olive oil, as needed for sautéing

3/4 teaspoon minced garlic

2 pinches grated ginger

1/2 cup sliced mushrooms

1/2 cup oyster mushrooms in pieces

1 red bell pepper, roasted, peeled and cut into
2" strips

1 yellow bell pepper, roasted, peeled and cut into
2" strips

3 tablespoons chopped cilantro leaves

2 small red tomatoes, peeled, seeded and diced

Salt and freshly ground black pepper to taste

3 ounces cold unsalted butter

Additional chopped cilantro leaves for garnish

Dredge filets in seasoned flour. Dip in egg and milk mixture, then back in flour. Shake off excess flour. Heat olive oil to medium in a large sauté pan or divide between 2 smaller pans. Sauté filets until golden then turn and finish cooking, taking care not to overcook. This should take about 8 minutes. Transfer to serving dish and place in warm spot while preparing sauce.

In the sauté pan(s) add the remainder of the ingredients except the butter. Sweat the mixture for 3 to 4 minutes, then incorporate butter at the last minute. Top the snapper with the sauce and serve immediately, garnished with additional fresh cilantro.

FRIED GOAT CHEESE WITH SUN-DRIED TOMATO VINAIGRETTE AND YELLOW TOMATO SALSA

Serves 4 as a first course

INGREDIENTS

1 egg

1/2 cup heavy cream

4 2-1/2-ounce rounds of goat cheese

1/2 cup all purpose flour

1/2 cup toasted sliced almonds

2 cups fresh bread crumbs

Vegetable oil for frying

1/2 cup shredded radicchio or other greens

Sun-Dried Tomato Vinaigrette (recipe follows)

Yellow Tomato Salsa (recipe follows)

To prepare goat cheese:

Combine the egg and cream in a bowl and mix well. Press the goat cheese rounds into the toasted almonds until both sides are coated. Dust each round with flour and dip into the egg/cream wash. Roll in the bread crumbs until both sides are completely covered. Place the breaded cheeses in a single layer on a large plate, cover and refrigerate for 2 hours or overnight.

SUN-DRIED TOMATO VINAIGRETTE

1/4 cup sun dried tomatoes (place tomatoes in a small
    bowl and add warm water to cover, allowing the
    tomatoes to soak until soft, about 1/2 hour)

1 sprig fresh thyme, leaves only

1 small clove garlic

1 leaf fresh basil

1/4 teaspoon salt

1 teaspoon sugar

2 tablespoons red wine vinegar

1 tablespoon balsamic vinegar

1/2 cup olive oil

Freshly ground black pepper

Place the reconstituted tomatoes in a food processor and purée. Press puréed tomatoes through a fine sieve to remove seeds and skin. Return the tomato mixture to the processor and add all the ingredients except the olive oil and pepper. Start the processor and slowly add the olive oil. Continue to process until the dressing is smooth and thick. Add black pepper to taste.

YELLOW TOMATO SALSA

1 large ripe yellow tomato, diced

2 large leaves fresh basil, sliced in chiffonade

1 small red bell pepper, roasted and peeled—dice
    half and cut other half into strips. Reserve strips
    for garnish

1 small clove garlic, minced
1 teaspoon shallot, minced
1 tablespoon balsamic vinegar
1 tablespoon extra virgin olive oil
Salt and freshly ground pepper to taste

In a small bowl combine the vinegar, garlic, and shallot, then whisk in the olive oil. Toss this with the remaining ingredients and season lightly with salt and freshly ground pepper. Can be made one day ahead, but bring to room temperature before serving.

To serve:

Heat oil in a deep cast iron or heavy metal skillet. Fry the cold breaded goat cheeses until golden brown. Drain on paper towels and keep warm. Pour some vinaigrette on each serving plate and place a warm fried goat cheese on top. Garnish with shredded radicchio, yellow tomato salsa and remaining roasted red pepper strips and serve with warm crusty bread.

TAMARA MURPHY

CAMPAGNE
SEATTLE

◈

Tamara Murphy, born in North Carolina, has been working in restaurants since she was 16. Trained in New York, Tamara moved to Seattle in 1988 to serve as sous chef under Dominique Place. In 1989, she represented the West Coast as one of twelve finalists in the prestigious Bocuse d'Or Competition, the only woman to be so honored. She assumed the position of executive chef at Campagne in 1990, was nominated for Rising Star Chef of the Year by The James Beard Foundation in 1991 and named one of the Ten Best New Chefs in America by *Food & Wine* in 1994. Tamara was honored as Best American Chef: Pacific Northwest in 1995 by The James Beard Foundation. The simplicity and directness of her presentations belie her technical mastery and the complex layering of flavors, textures and colors that characterize her dishes. Tamara's cooking has received excellent reviews in *Gourmet, The Atlantic, Esquire, Bon Appétit, Condé Nast Traveler* and *Travel & Leisure*.

Campagne, which is located just a few steps up the hill from the Pike Place Market, enjoys a view of Elliot Bay, as well as the flower stalls and produce stands of the market. The menu takes its inspiration from the sun-drenched cuisine of Provence, but uses the exquisite produce, seafood and game of the Pacific Northwest. In the summer of 1994, owners Peter and Maria Lewis opened their much-awaited café and charcuterie on Post Alley, just below the restaurant.

Some of Tamara's signature dishes are calamari dusted with ground almonds, sautéed in olive oil and served with fresh thyme and lemon; seafood sausage sautéed and served with a tomato saffron coulis; *pissaladière*, free-range chicken stuffed under the skin with goat cheese and served with roasted garlic sauce; and scallops, pan-roasted and served on a light potato purée with a green peppercorn, tarragon and lemon nage. All of these creations, like her version of the classic Provençal fish stew which follows, would be outstanding with Pinot Gris.

Provençal Fish Soup with Rouille

Serves 6

*The key to success with this dish is in the selection of seafood:
only the freshest will do. The amounts and variety are up to
you, but figure about 7 or 8 ounces per person. For visual as
well as gustatory interest, select a combination of white fish,
salmon and shellfish. In testing the recipe, we used 1/2 pound
salmon filet, 1 pound halibut filet, 1/2 pound spot prawns and
1 pound mussels for 6 people.*

Ingredients

1 leek (white part only), cut in julienne strips

1 ounce fennel bulb, cut into thin slivers lengthwise

Assorted vegetables, depending on the season, such
    as new potatoes, asparagus, peas, turnips, carrots,
    etc., cut into attractive shapes

Fish Fumet (recipe to follow)

3 pounds fresh fish, prepared in attractive
    bite-sized pieces (cover and refrigerate until
    ready to assemble)

Pinch of saffron

1 tablespoon lemon juice

1 tablespoon chopped parsley

1 tablespoon butter

Salt and white pepper to taste

6 toasted French bread croutons

Rouille (recipe to follow)

Blanch vegetables until just *al dente* and set aside.
Bring fish fumet to a boil. Turn the heat down to a
simmer and add selected seafood and vegetables.
Poach until fish is just done, 5 to 10 minutes
depending on the type of fish. Remove from pot and
arrange in large flat soup bowls. Finish broth with
saffron, lemon juice, parsley, butter, salt and pepper
and ladle over fish. Garnish by floating a toasted
French bread crouton topped lavishly with rouille.

Fish Fumet

2 pounds white fish bones (ask your seafood store
    for parts for stock)

1 onion

1 leek (white part only)

1 celery rib

2-1/2 ounces of fennel bulb

7 ounces white wine

6 coriander seeds

5 black peppercorns

Sprig of fresh thyme

Rinse fish bones under cold running water. Chop
into small, manageable pieces. Peel or trim onions,
leeks, celery and fennel. Chop into a small dice. In a
large saucepan combine vegetables, wine, spices and

thyme. Bring to a simmer, cover and allow to sweat for 8 to 10 minutes. Add fish bones and just enough cold water to cover bones. Bring to a boil, reduce heat to a simmer and cook for 20 minutes. Be sure to skim any impurities which rise to the surface. Strain through a fine sieve and then strain again through cheesecloth to obtain a clear stock. Makes about 12 cups.

Rouille

1 egg yolk
1 teaspoon Dijon mustard
1 teaspoon lemon juice

1 tablespoon red pepper purée (roast 1/2 red bell
    pepper on top of grill or gas burner or under
    broiler until skin blisters, cool, remove skin and
    seeds and purée in food processor)
1/4 to 1/2 cup good fruity olive oil

Put all ingredients in food processor except olive oil. Purée, then with machine running, very slowly add just enough olive oil to make a nice mayonnaise. Season to taste with salt and pepper.

RADEK CERNY

PAPILLON CAFÉ
DENVER

◈

Radek Cerny was born in Prague, Czechoslovakia, the son of a farming family whose property was seized during the Communist takeover in 1948. He chose cooking as a career in his native country, then tried in vain for many years to obtain a visa for study and travel abroad. Desperate for better opportunities, he joined a tour group to Yugoslavia. He was able to slip away and get to the Italian border, where he made a dramatic midnight escape across the frontier, eluding the Yugoslavian patrols. Radek was given asylum by the Italian government and was able to arrange for sponsorship and a job in the United States in 1979.

Upon arriving in the United States, Cerny began working at restaurants in the Denver area. In 1987, Cerny studied with Roger Vergé at the Moulin de Mougins in Provence. He returned to work with Vergé in the summer of 1988, and in 1989 he worked under Jean-Georges Vongerichten at the Lafayette Restaurant in New York. Later in 1989, he started his own restaurant, The European Café in Boulder, Colorado, which has been honored with a top rating in the *Zagat Guide*. He opened The European Café in downtown Denver in 1991. In 1993, Radek was included in a Culinary Gala at L'Oasis in La Napoule, France, where he worked with such luminaries as Alain Ducasse, Gerard Boyer, Louis Outhier, Jacques Maximin, Michel Bras and Roger Vergé. In the spring of 1994, The European Café was chosen to host a luncheon honoring French Master Chef, Paul Bocuse, with the proceeds from the packed house going to the Colorado AIDS Project. In 1995 The European Café was renamed Papillon Café.

Radek's Lobster Fricassee with Paprika is an almost ideal companion for Pinot Gris. The richness of the lobster and the slightly sweet anise flavors of the tarragon and chervil pair splendidly with the wine.

Lobster Fricassee with Paprika

Serves 4

Ingredients

4 live lobsters, about 1-1/2 pounds each
3 tablespoons chopped shallots
2 tablespoons unsalted butter
1 tablespoon sweet paprika
1 tablespoon tomato paste
4 tablespoons Cognac
1 cup dry white wine
3 sprigs fresh tarragon
2-1/4 cups heavy cream
2 tablespoons chopped chervil
Salt and freshly cracked black pepper

Prepare each lobster by piercing the head between the eyes with a sharp pointed knife. (For an alternative method see page 52.) Cut each lobster in half, lengthwise, discarding the intestinal tract. If there is coral in any of the lobsters, remove it and reserve it for use later in the recipe.

Sauté the shallots in the butter until they are just softened, using a skillet that will be large enough to hold the lobsters comfortably. Add the paprika and tomato paste to the pan, stirring to combine.

Place the lobsters, shell side up, in the hot mixture and cook briefly over medium heat. Add the Cognac and flame. Turn the lobsters over and add the wine and tarragon. Cover the pan tightly and simmer over low heat for about 20 minutes, checking to make sure the liquid doesn't all cook away.

Take the pan from the heat and remove the lobsters. Using a towel to protect your hands, take the tail meat and claw meat from the shell, removing each section in one piece if possible. Divide the meat among four plates or shallow soup plates and set aside in a warm place.

Return the skillet to the stove and, over medium high heat, reduce the sauce by half. Stir in the heavy cream and bring the sauce to a gentle boil for a few minutes until it has thickened slightly. Stir in any reserved coral and salt and pepper to taste. Using a fine sieve, strain the sauce into a clean saucepan and return to low heat until just warmed through. Pour the sauce over the lobster meat and sprinkle with the chopped chervil.

JAIME D'OLIVEIRA

THE CAPITAL GRILLE
PROVIDENCE, BOSTON, WASHINGTON D.C.

❖

Jaime D'Oliveira is currently executive chef and director of menu development for The Capital Grille organization, which he joined in the fall of 1993. Earlier, he served as chef and general manager at Angel's, as executive chef at Alforno's, and as general manager/maitre d' at The Arboretum, all in the Providence area.

The first Capital Grille made its debut in Providence in 1990, followed by another on Newbury Street in Boston. A third Capital Grille opened in Washington D.C. in the fall of 1994. The restaurants feature lavishly furnished interiors with brass, marble, plush carpeting, fine wood panelling, paintings and sculpture, evoking the feeling of an elegant private club. There are open kitchens, special facilities for on-premises dry-aging of meats, and a glassed-in wine room for storing the extensive collection that has earned The Capital Grille the Best of Award of Excellence from *Wine Spectator*.

In 1996 The Capital Grille will be opening restaurants in Chestnut Hill, Massachusetts; Troy, Michigan; Miami, Florida; and Houston, Texas.

While The Capital Grille is justly famous for its beef, the menu features an extensive array of seafood from the North Atlantic. Jaime's recipe for Creamy Scallop, Corn and Garlic Soup is reminiscent of the traditional chowders of the region. We liked the way the sweet tones of the corn and garlic and the succulence of the scallops married with the rich fruit character of Pinot Gris, while the citrus flavors of the wine and the spicy touch of cayenne in the soup provided delightful accents.

CREAMY SCALLOP, CORN AND GARLIC SOUP

Serves 6

INGREDIENTS

1 large head of garlic (about 20 large cloves)
  separated into cloves with any green germ
  removed from each

4 cups rich fish stock or clam juice

2 large russet potatoes, peeled and cut into
  1/2-inch cubes

1 cup heavy cream

2 cups fresh yellow corn, cut from the cob (about 3
  ears) and blanched for 1 minute

1 pound bay scallops or sea scallops (if using sea
  scallops, cut in half crosswise)

Salt to taste

6 pats unsalted butter

Cayenne pepper

1 tablespoon finely minced Italian parsley

1 tablespoon separated chive flowers

Place the garlic cloves in a large heavy-bottomed
saucepan and cover with 2 cups of the fish stock.

Bring to a boil over medium heat. Reduce heat to low
and cook garlic, covered, until soft, about 10 minutes.
Add the potatoes and cook, covered, until soft, about
15 more minutes.

Purée the mixture in a food processor or blender
and return to the saucepan. Add the remaining
2 cups of fish stock and the cream, and cook, over
medium heat, whisking slowly but steadily, until
slightly thickened, about 10 minutes. Do not let
the soup boil.

Add the scallops. Cook until the scallops are tender,
about 4 minutes. Season the soup with salt.

To assemble:
Put a spoonful of corn in the center of each bowl.
Using a slotted spoon, arrange the scallops on top
of the corn. Pour the broth around. Place a pat of
butter on top of the scallops in the middle of the
bowl, then sprinkle with the cayenne pepper,
chopped parsley and chive flowers.

CHRISTOPHER ISRAEL

ZEFIRO
PORTLAND, OREGON

❖

*L*ike many of our contributing chefs, Christopher Israel's interest in food began at home. He grew up in a large family in San Diego and was inspired by his mother's passion for cooking. During and after his studies toward a B.A. in art history at Berkeley, he worked in various Bay Area restaurants, usually as a host or server. It was as the host at Square One in San Francisco that he met Joyce Goldstein, who was to become a friend and important mentor. In the four years he worked there he learned to appreciate her pan-Mediterranean approach to food, which includes the flavors of North Africa, the Middle East, Greece, and Turkey, as well those of the European coast. Christopher drew on this influence, plus his belief in simple but meticulous preparation, when he opened Zefiro in 1990 with partner Bruce Carey.

Zefiro is a stylish restaurant—a combination of Mediterranean simplicity and high design. The amber stucco walls are adorned with just a few black and white photographs. Heavy gold velvet drapes hang by the entry and behind the banquettes, reminding one of a Venetian palazzo but functioning as baffles for the lively ambiance. A copper-covered bar, flower arrangements perched on columns and ledges, and large wire urns filled with seasonal fruit add color and light.

In its first year of operation, Zefiro was named Restaurant of the Year by *The Oregonian* and given four stars in *Northwest Best Places*. It has also been featured in *Gourmet*, *The New York Times* and *The Atlantic* and received the top ranking in the Zagat Survey and the 1995 DiRoNa award.

Recent ventures include Zero, a tiny space dedicated to exquisite ice creams and sorbets, breakfast pastries and rustic breads and Sauce Box, a hip downtown spot for contemporary music and tasty bar food.

Lamb Stew with Artichokes, Olives, Tomatoes and Pinot Gris, Garnished with Gremolata

Serves 4

Ingredients

2 tablespoons olive oil

2 pounds lamb, cut from the leg into 1-1/2 inch cubes

2 small onions, cut into 1/4 inch dice

1/2 cup puréed tomatoes (preferably canned Italian
  pear tomatoes that have been drained and seeded)

1 cup Pinot Gris

2 teaspoons chopped fresh rosemary
  (1 teaspoon dried)

3 cloves garlic, finely minced

1/2 cup black olives (oil-cured recommended,
  pitted or not, depending on your preference)

Olive oil for sautéing artichokes

12 baby artichokes (or substitute 3 globe artichokes,
  trimmed down to the heart, bottom and a little bit
  of stem; or canned artichoke hearts)

Gremolata

1/4 cup finely chopped parsley

1 tablespoon finely chopped lemon zest

1-1/2 teaspoon minced garlic

Combine ingredients in a small bowl. Cover with
plastic wrap and refrigerate until ready to use.

Preheat oven to 300 degrees.

Sprinkle the lamb cubes with salt and pepper.
In an ovenproof and flameproof casserole, brown
the lamb in olive oil over medium high heat.
Don't crowd the lamb; sauté in small batches if
necessary, removing it to a warm plate as it
browns. When all the lamb has been browned,
add the onion to the pan and sauté until just
wilted. Add the minced garlic, tomatoes, rosemary
and Pinot Gris. Turn up the heat and add the
lamb back to the casserole. Season with salt and
pepper. When the mixture comes to a boil, cover
the casserole and move it to the oven. Cook for
1-1/2 hours. Add the olives and continue cooking
until the meat is fork tender, half an hour to an
hour longer.

While the lamb is braising, trim the artichokes,
cutting about 1/2 inch off the top and tidying
the stem. Peel away the darker outer leaves and
with a paring knife clean up the heart. Cut the
artichoke into quarters (or halves if the artichoke
is very small) and place in a bowl with water
that has a few drops of lemon juice in it to prevent

discoloring. When all of the artichokes have been cleaned, drain, then sauté in a little olive oil until tender. Remove from the pan with a slotted spoon and spread on a cookie sheet to cool quickly. When the lamb is done, remove the casserole from the oven and stir in the artichokes. Taste for salt and pepper and season accordingly.

Serve with soft polenta, boiled new potatoes or grilled bread, and sprinkle liberally with gremolata.

An excellent beginning to this meal would be a salad of arugula, orange and fennel with a hot pepper oil and lemon juice dressing. For dessert, fresh strawberries and marscarpone.

Roast Salmon with Sweet and Sour Onion Confit, served with Sautéed Spinach and Deep-Fried Polenta Croutons

Serves 4

This is a Venetian-inspired dish of salmon with sweet and sour onions, raisins and pine nuts. While traditionally done with sole that has been marinated overnight, then fried, we like the sweet and sour flavors with the rich taste of the salmon. It is a perfect foil for Pinot Gris. The spinach and polenta round out this dish for an elegant meal. Make the polentra the night before and this dish is put together in less than an hour.

Ingredients

4 6-ounce salmon filets
Olive oil for coating salmon and sautéing
    polenta and spinach
Salt and freshly ground black pepper
1 pound cleaned spinach leaves
Sweet and Sour Onion Confit (recipe follows)
Polenta Croutons (recipe follows)

Sweet and Sour Onion Confit

2 large yellow onions
1 tablespoon butter
2 tablespoons olive oil
1-1/2 cup dry white wine
1/2 cup white wine vinegar
1/4 cup raisins
1 tablespoon sugar
3 bay leaves

12 or so black peppercorns
Salt and pepper to taste
1/4 cup toasted pine nuts (for garnish)

Sauté onions in butter and oil over medium heat until wilted, soft and slightly golden, about 15 minutes. Add the remaining ingredients except the pine nuts and simmer for 15 minutes. Turn off heat and keep warm. Taste again for salt and pepper.

Polenta Croutons

4 cups cold water
1 cup polenta or coarse cornmeal
Salt to taste
1/4 cup unsalted butter
1/2 cup Parmesan cheese, freshly grated

In a heavy-bottomed saucepan, stir the cold water and polenta together. Cook over medium low heat, stirring every few minutes to prevent sticking, until it is thick, smooth and no longer tastes raw or grainy. This will take 25 to 30 minutes. Stir in butter and Parmesan and taste for seasoning. Spoon the hot mixture into a well buttered loaf pan and chill in the refrigerator overnight.

To make croutons, unmold polenta, cut into 1″ slices, then cut each slice into squares.

Preheat oven to 450 degrees.

Lightly oil, salt and pepper the salmon and roast until done, approximately 7 to 10 minutes. Meanwhile fry the polenta croutons in olive oil until golden brown and crispy. Drain on paper towels. Sauté the spinach in olive oil with a little salt and pepper until just wilted. Set aside covered until ready to use. When the salmon is done, remove from oven.

To assemble:

Divide the spinach among four dinner plates, placing it in the center. Put a salmon filet on top of the spinach and spoon some Sweet and Sour Onion Confit over the fish. Place 3 polenta croutons on each plate and garnish the dish with a sprinkling of toasted pine nuts on top of the onion mixture.

Suggestions for starting this meal are chilled oysters on the half shell, chilled asparagus with lemon aïoli and capers, prosciutto with figs or melon, or a simple salad of arugula and radicchio with balsamic vinaigrette. For dessert Christopher recommends a chocolate-hazelnut semifreddo or a pear tart with vanilla ice cream.

Stu Stein

Riviera
Atlanta

*S*tu Stein grew up on the north side of Chicago and started to work in restaurants as a teenager. He attended the University of Illinois at Champagne-Urbana where he received a B.S. in business with a minor in music performance. After graduation, Stu moved back to Chicago to pursue his first love: cooking. He worked in various kitchens around Chicago, then had the good fortune to work at St. Germain under the direction of Larry Smith and Michel Maloiseau. He also returned to school to get a degree in Culinary Arts from the Culinary School of Kendall College.

Stu then served as sous chef under Jean-Claude Poilevey at La Fontaine (later to be called Jean-Claude's). During the two years he spent under Jean-Claude's guidance, he won the Champagne Mumm Competition for Culinary Excellence. The prize included two months in France studying and working with legendary chefs Paul Bocuse and Francis Garcia. Upon his return from France, he worked under Jean Banchet (of Le Français in Wheeling, Illinois) at Ciboulette, his new restaurant in Atlanta. While there, Stu taught at the Culinary School of the Art Institute of Atlanta and won a silver medal in the 1993 Georgia Seafood Challenge. In March of 1994, Stu assumed the duties of chef de cuisine at Café Allegro in Kansas City. Stu was the Midwest regional winner of the *Gourmet*/Evian Healthy Menu Awards in 1995.

In 1995 he returned to Atlanta to assist Jean Banchet in opening Riviera and stayed on as chef de cuisine. Riviera, a French restaurant with an emphasis on Mediterranean flavors, has been featured in recent articles in *Gourmet* and *The New York Times*.

PAN ROASTED QUAIL WITH SHIITAKE MUSHROOMS AND CARAMELIZED GARLIC

Serves 4 as an entrée or 8 as a first course

INGREDIENTS

2 to 3 tablespoons olive oil, plus 1/4 cup for
    sautéing quail

24 medium garlic cloves, peeled

16 medium shiitake mushrooms, quartered

1 tomato, peeled, seeded and finely diced

12 ounces dried cherries, macerated for an hour
    in 1/4 cup brandy

8 quail, whole or with the breast bone removed

1 cup flour for dredging

Salt and black pepper

1/2 medium orange, zest only, cut into thin strips

1/2 tablespoon whole white peppercorns

4 ounces dry white wine

3/4 cup game stock, or substitute a dark, rich
    chicken stock

6 sprigs winter savory, leaves stripped

4 tablespoons cold butter, cut into small pieces

8 1/2-inch slices polenta, brushed lightly with olive
    oil, then grilled (see recipe on page 102)

Preheat oven to 500 degrees.

In a very hot skillet, heat 1 to 2 tablespoons olive oil, then add the garlic cloves and caramelize quickly. Remove garlic and set aside. Put a little additional olive oil in the pan and, when hot, add the shiitakes, tomato, cherries and caramelized garlic. Sauté two minutes and remove.

Season each quail with salt and freshly ground black pepper inside and out. Stuff each quail with the mushroom mixture and truss, then lightly dust with flour. In a large skillet heat 1/4 cup olive oil until hot. Add quail breast side down. Sauté until dark golden brown, then turn and brown on each side. Place skillet in preheated oven and roast the quail for 5 to 7 minutes. Remove quail to a warm spot while you make the sauce.

In the same skillet, combine the orange zest and peppercorns. Add the wine and reduce until almost all liquid has evaporated. Add the stock and reduce by half. Add the winter savory and remove skillet from the heat. Begin adding the butter a bit at a time, incorporating it with a whisk as you go. Correct seasoning for salt.

To serve:
Place grilled polenta in center of four warm plates. Arrange two quail on each bed of polenta. With a spoon, drizzle the sauce around the quail and polenta and garnish with whole Italian parsley leaves.

Anthony Sindt

TONY SINDACO

MAYFAIR GRILLE
COCONUT GROVE, FLORIDA

❖

Tony Sindaco grew up in the kitchen of his very Italian grandmother in the Pocono Mountains of Pennsylvania. As a child, while his brothers were at the playground, he preferred to be with his grandmother learning how to make noodles, how to choose perfect ripe tomatoes and how to use fresh herbs. He started out bussing tables in local resort hotels when he was 14 and by age 17 had decided to become a chef. Tony achieved his culinary education under the European system, serving a four-year American Culinary Federation certified apprenticeship under chef René Mettler at the Buckhill Inn and in Switzerland. He learned all of the posts in the traditional brigade and served as chef tournant at the Palace Hotel under master chef Henry Jolidon and as chef poissonnier at the Helmsley Palace under chef André René.

Tony rose through the kitchen hierarchy in a variety of hotels and resorts, serving as executive chef at the Nassau Inn in Princeton, the Georgetown Hotel in Washington D.C., Loew's Ventana Canyon Resort in Arizona, and the Doral Telluride Resort in Colorado. During this period he was also team captain for French gold medal teams at the 1982 and 1983 New York Food Shows and won three silver medals and one bronze medal at the 1984 and 1988 International Culinary Olympics in Frankfurt, Germany. He represented the state of New York in the American Seafood Challenge and was a guest chef at the James Beard Foundation in 1989.

Tony is currently executive chef at the Mayfair Grille, an elegant resort restaurant in Coconut Grove with a menu based on the seasonal and regional ingredients of Florida.

CRAB CROQUETTES WITH
BLACK BEAN-CORN RELISH AND
RED CHILE VINAIGRETTE

Serves 4 (12 croquettes)

INGREDIENTS

CRAB CROQUETTES

1/2 pound crab meat

5 ounces russet potatoes, peeled

1 egg yolk

1-1/2 tablespoons cracker crumbs or bread crumbs

1-1/2 tablespoons chives, chopped

1-1/2 tablespoons Italian parsley, chopped

1-1/2 tablespoons chervil (if not available,
   substitute an additional 2 teaspoons each of
   chives and parsley)

2 teaspoons fresh dill weed, chopped

1 teaspoon Dijon mustard

1 teaspoon fresh lemon juice

Salt and pepper to taste

Peanut oil for frying

Clean crab meat of any shells. Dice potatoes and cook in salted water until tender. Drain potatoes and put into small mixing bowl. Add the egg yolk to the potatoes and whip until smooth. In mixing bowl, combine potato mixture and cracker crumbs, then add all other ingredients including crab meat until all are well incorporated and form a ball. For each croquette, weigh out 2 ounces of crab mixture and form into log

shape. Reserve croquettes in the refrigerator until ready to bread.

BREADING

3/4 cup cracker crumbs or bread crumbs

1 tablespoon flour

1 egg

1 tablespoon water

Put cracker crumbs in a shallow dish. Put flour in another shallow dish. Combine egg and water in another shallow dish. Dredge croquettes in the flour, the egg mixture and then the crumbs. Put the formed and breaded croquettes on a baking sheet and chill in the refrigerator until ready to fry.

BLACK BEAN-CORN RELISH

3/4 cup black beans, cooked

1 tablespoon olive oil for sautéeing

1 cup corn kernels

1/2 teaspoon minced garlic

1/2 plum tomato, peeled, seeded and diced

1/2 red bell pepper, roasted, peeled and diced

3 tablespoons cilantro, chopped

3 tablespoons extra virgin olive oil

1 tablespoon red wine vinegar

2 teaspoons Worcestershire sauce
Juice of 1/2 lime
Salt and pepper to taste

Cook black beans until tender, then let cool in the cooking water (good quality canned black beans may be substituted). Drain the beans and measure out 3/4 cup.

Sauté the corn kernels in olive oil until tender. Add minced garlic and cook thoroughly, but do not permit to brown. Combine all ingredients in a mixing bowl and gently toss to combine. Reserve.

RED CHILE VINAIGRETTE
1/2 teaspoon garlic, finely chopped
2 large egg yolks
1/2 cup chile oil (recipe follows)
2 tablespoons plus 1 teaspoon red wine vinegar
Juice of 1/2 lemon
Worcestershire sauce to taste
Salt and pepper to taste

Sweat garlic with a little olive oil and set aside to cool. Whisk the egg yolks and the cooled garlic together in a small bowl. Whisk the chile oil in drop by drop until it emulsifies. Slowly whisk in the vinegar until completely incorporated. Season with the lemon juice, Worcestershire sauce and salt and pepper to taste.

To make chile oil:
Combine 1 ounce chile powder and enough water to make a paste. Put 1/2 cup vegetable oil, 1/2 cup olive oil and the chile powder paste in a blender container and blend on high speed for 30 seconds. Pour the mixture into a saucepan and warm, stirring occasionally, then allow the solids to settle out. Repeat several times, then strain into a sterilized container. The chile oil will keep for months. Other seasoned oils, such as curry oil or herbes de Provence oil, can be made using the same method.

To assemble:
Deep fry croquettes in peanut oil until golden brown. Drain on paper towels. Arrange croquettes in the center of the serving plate, spoon Black Bean-Corn Relish around and drizzle with the Red Chile Vinaigrette. Garnish with lime wedges and cilantro.

STEPHANIE PEARL KIMMEL

KING ESTATE WINERY
EUGENE, OREGON

◈

Although a native of Texas, Stephanie grew up living and travelling around the world. Her father was a career Air Force pilot who was stationed in Japan, Europe and North Africa, as well as in many regions of the United States. Her parents, both enthusiastic cooks and cultural explorers, engendered in her a love and appreciation for diverse culinary traditions.

Stephanie's formal education was in English literature and French cultural history, with degrees from the University of Oregon and the Sorbonne. As a graduate student in comparative literature, she took her first restaurant job to help pay for educational expenses, and it was there she discovered her real passion. Her life-long interest in cooking evolved into a métier. Using a well-worn copy of Julia Child's *The French Chef*, and inspired by Ms. Child's "you can do this too" attitude, she taught herself French technique by mastering the recipes in the book. In 1972, she opened the Excelsior Café in Eugene, Oregon, pioneering a Northwest culinary movement with the use of seasonal menus that celebrated the bounty of the region. The restaurant was also the first in Oregon to feature the wines of the young Oregon wine industry. During her tenure there as chef/owner, the Excelsior Café was featured in *Cook's Magazine*, *Food & Wine*, *Gourmet*, *Travel and Leisure*, *Bon Appétit*, *Sunset*, *Nation's Restaurant News* and many other national, regional and local publications.

After selling the restaurant in the spring of 1993, Stephanie took an extended trip to France to explore regional markets and vineyards. In September of 1993 she joined the team at King Estate as culinary director. Her responsibilities include preparing meals for guests; research, recipe testing, and writing the Pinot Gris cookbook; supervising the planning and implementation of a full-scale hospitality program; working with the nursery manager and gardeners on planning and planting the organic vegetable and flower garden, berry patches and orchards; and the development of a line of King Estate food products.

Pizzetta with Walla Walla Sweet Onions, Saffron, New Potatoes, Anchovies, Olives, and Thyme

Serves 4 as individual luncheon pizzas

Ingredients

1 batch Pizza Dough (recipe follows)

1/4 cup olive oil

4 medium Walla Walla sweet onions (or other sweet yellow or white onion), sliced thin

2 cloves garlic, roughly chopped

1/4 teaspoon saffron threads, crumbled fine

1/2 teaspoon chopped fresh thyme leaves, plus another 1/2 teaspoon for garnish

Salt and freshly ground pepper to taste

4 small new potatoes, boiled in their jackets, cooled, peeled and sliced in rounds

4 anchovy filets, rinsed well and patted dry, then cut into thin slivers

12 Mediterranean-style olives (such as Kalamata), pitted and cut into slivers

Pizza Dough

1 package (2 teaspoons) active dry yeast

1 teaspoon sugar

1/2 cup plus 2 tablespoons warm water (105 to 120 degrees)

1 cup plus 2 tablespoons unbleached all purpose flour

1/2 cup rye flour

3/4 teaspoon salt

2 teaspoons vegetable oil

1 to 2 tablespoons cornmeal for pans or stone

Stir the yeast and sugar into the warm water and let stand 10 minutes. Using a food processor fitted with the metal blade, put the two kinds of flour and the salt in the work bowl and turn the machine on. With the machine running, pour the yeast mixture through the feed tube and process for about 45 seconds, or until the dough pulls away from the sides of the bowl. Add the oil through the feed tube and process for 60 seconds longer.

Preheat oven to 400 degrees.

Divide the dough into four parts. On a floured surface, roll the dough into four circles. Sprinkle cornmeal on baking sheets. Transfer the dough to the baking sheets and set in a warm place while you proceed with making the onion topping.

WALLA WALLA SWEET ONION TOPPING

Heat olive oil in a sauté pan over medium heat. Add the onions and garlic and cook, stirring occasionally, until the onions start to give up their juices, about 10 minutes. It is very important not to brown the onions. Add 1/4 teaspoon crumbled saffron threads and continue to cook down until all of the juices have evaporated and the onions are very tender and golden in hue. This will take about half an hour. Add thyme and salt and pepper to taste. Set aside to cool slightly.

To assemble each pizzetta:

Spread the saffron onion mixture evenly over the surface of the pizza dough. Place the cooked potato rounds on top of the onion mixture. Place the anchovy strips and olives around the potatoes in a decorative pattern. Drizzle the potatoes with a touch of olive oil and scatter the remaining 1/2 teaspoon thyme over the surface of the pizzetta. Bake for 15-20 minutes, or until the crust is puffed and golden.

SMOKED SALMON MOUSSE

Serves 12-16 as hors d'oeuvres

This is a perfect party recipe—very elegant, yet simple to make with a food processor. Smoked Salmon Mousse can be served as spread for crackers or French bread toast rounds, or, using a pastry bag with a decorative tip, you can pipe the mixture onto cucumber rounds or toast rounds. Garnish with a tiny dollop of sour cream topped with a caper or a small sprig of dill. This mousse never fails to draw raves, and it goes perfectly with a glass of Pinot Gris.

INGREDIENTS

12 ounces *dry* smoked salmon (not lox)

1 tablespoon plus 2 teaspoons strained lemon juice

2 tablespoons chopped shallot or the white part
   of a scallion

2 teaspoons fresh dill weed or 1 teaspoon dried
   dill weed

3/4 cup melted butter, cooled

1 cup sour cream

Break up the smoked salmon pieces with your hands to feel for any bones and to remove the skin. Weigh out 12 ounces of flaked smoked salmon and put it in the work bowl of a food processor fitted with the metal blade. Add the shallots, dill, and lemon juice and process until smooth. With the machine running, slowly pour in the cooled melted butter until it is incorporated. With a rubber spatula, transfer the smoked salmon mixture to a medium size bowl. Gently fold in the sour cream until completely incorporated.

If serving as a spread, transfer to serving bowl immediately and refrigerate covered until just before you are ready to serve. If you are going to pipe the mousse with a pastry bag, it is best to let the mixture set up by refrigerating for an hour. The mousse can be made up to 3 days ahead.

BRAISED RABBIT WITH PANCETTA, MUSHROOMS AND TARRAGON

Serves 4

INGREDIENTS

7 tablespoons unsalted butter

1 large rabbit fryer (about 3-1/2 pounds) cut into
    6 pieces (reserve liver)

Salt and freshly ground pepper

2 tablespoons finely chopped shallots or green onions

1 cup dry white wine

1 cup chicken stock

1 branch fresh tarragon, about 4 inches long

2 bay leaves

4 ounces pancetta (unsmoked Italian-style bacon that
    can be found at specialty markets, or substitute
    blanched salt pork), cut into 1/4-inch cubes

6 ounces pearl onions, blanched, trimmed and peeled

4 ounces mushrooms, trimmed, cleaned and sliced

2 tablespoons Dijon mustard

1 tablespoon chopped fresh tarragon leaves, plus
    additional for garnish

1 tablespoon chopped Italian parsley

In a medium flame-proof casserole or Dutch oven, melt 2 tablespoons butter over medium-high heat. Add the rabbit pieces and brown on all sides, removing the pieces to a plate in a warm spot as they brown. Salt and pepper to taste. Add another tablespoon of butter to the pot, add the shallots and sauté until translucent. Add the wine, scraping up any browned bits from the bottom of the pan with a wooden spatula. Add the chicken stock, the branch of tarragon and the bay leaves. Return rabbit pieces to pan, bring the liquid to a simmer and braise, covered, for 25 to 30 minutes.

Meanwhile, in a sauté pan over medium-low heat, melt 1 tablespoon butter and add pancetta. Cook slowly, stirring frequently, until very lightly browned. Remove to drain on paper towels. Discard fat from pan and add 1 tablespoon of butter. Add pearl onions and cook, covered, over medium-low heat until tender. This will take about 20 minutes. Set aside in a warm spot.

In another sauté pan, melt 1 tablespoon butter. Add mushrooms and cook gently over medium heat until the mushrooms have reabsorbed their juices. Add the mushrooms to the pan with the pearl onions.

In the pan that the mushrooms were cooked in, melt remaining 1 tablespoon butter. Season the liver with salt and pepper and sauté briefly, about 2 minutes on each side. Keep warm.

When the rabbit is done, remove the rabbit pieces from the casserole and hold, covered, in a warm place. Discard the bay leaves and the tarragon branch. Whisk in mustard and boil rapidly until the braising liquid is reduced to a sauce-like consistency.

Adjust seasoning. Reduce the heat to low. Add the pancetta, pearl onions, and mushrooms to the casserole and stir to combine. Add the rabbit pieces back to the casserole and turn to coat evenly with the sauce. Ladle some of the sauce on the liver to coat and slice into four pieces. Place the rabbit pieces and the liver on a platter and spoon the sauce around.

This is a delightful dish for spring, made with morels and served with egg noodles and asparagus or fiddlehead ferns. A variation we do for summer substitutes basil or summer savory for the tarragon and is served with new potatoes, tiny green beans and yellow and red cherry tomatoes. In the fall, try using chanterelle mushrooms and thyme accompanied by puréed root vegetables.

Salmon-Corn Cakes with Lemon Aïoli and Tomato, Corn and Basil Salsa

Serves 4

Ingredients

1-1/2 cups dry white wine

1-1/2 cups water

10 black peppercorns

2-inch strip lemon peel

2 sprigs parsley

1 pound salmon filet

1/2 cup green onions, finely chopped

1/2 cup red bell pepper, finely diced

1/2 cup celery, finely diced

1 cup corn kernels, freshly shucked and blanched for
   2 minutes in boiling water and drained

2 tablespoons fresh basil, finely chopped

2 tablespoons parsley, finely chopped

3/4 cup good quality mayonnaise (homemade or
   Best Foods/Hellman's)

1 teaspoon Dijon mustard

1/4 teaspoon Tabasco sauce

Salt and freshly ground pepper to taste

1 large egg, lightly beaten

1/4 cup fresh bread crumbs, plus bread crumbs for
   coating (about 1-1/2 cups total)

2 to 4 tablespoons olive oil for sautéing

Bring wine, water, peppercorns, lemon peel and parsley to a simmer in a large sauté pan. Add salmon, bring back to a simmer and poach for 8 to 10 minutes, or until just cooked through. Remove salmon with a slotted spatula and set aside to cool.

When cool, flake salmon into a mixing bowl, discarding any skin or bones. Add the green onions, red bell pepper, celery, corn, basil and parsley and gently combine. In a separate bowl, mix the mayonnaise, mustard and Tabasco. Fold into the salmon mixture, then salt and pepper to taste. Add the egg and 1/4-cup bread crumbs and mix to combine.

Form into 12 patties. Coat the patties with the remaining bread crumbs and set aside, refrigerated, until ready to sauté. (This can be done up to 2 hours ahead.)

Put 2 tablespoons of the olive oil in a sauté pan over medium heat. Taking care not to crowd, cook salmon-corn cakes in a single layer until golden brown, about 3 to 4 minutes on each side. Continue until all the cakes are done, adding more olive oil to the pan if needed. Serve with Lemon Aïoli and Tomato, Corn and Basil Salsa as accompaniments.

Lemon Aïoli

Large pinch salt

3 medium cloves garlic, peeled

1-1/2 tablespoons lemon juice

1 teaspoon grated lemon zest

1 large egg yolk, room temperature

1 cup olive oil

In a food processor, pulse the salt, garlic, lemon juice and lemon zest until smooth. Add egg yolk and pulse briefly to combine. With machine running, add olive oil in a thin drizzle until incorporated. If too thick, thin with a little hot water. Makes about 1 cup.

Tomato, Corn and Basil Salsa

2 tomatoes, seeded and diced

1/2 red onion, chopped

1 cup corn kernels, freshly shucked and blanched

1-1/2 teaspoons garlic, minced

1 teaspoon lemon juice

12 large leaves basil, cut in fine chiffonade

1/4 cup parsley, chopped

Salt and freshly ground pepper to taste

Combine all ingredients and toss lightly. This should be assembled as close to serving time as possible.

Scallops Wrapped in Smoked Salmon with Caviar and Beurre Blanc

Serves 4 as first course

Ingredients

12 large sea scallops, muscles removed

12 3- to 4-inch strips of cold-smoked salmon,
approximately 1-inch wide (lox can be substituted)

Beurre Blanc (recipe follows)

1 tablespoon unsalted butter

1 teaspoon lemon zest, finely chopped

1 tablespoon chives, finely chopped

1/2 teaspoon red lumpfish caviar

Wrap each scallop with a strip of smoked salmon and secure with a wooden toothpick. Refrigerate, covered, until ready to assemble. This can be done up to 2 hours ahead. Meanwhile, make Beurre Blanc.

Beurre Blanc

1-1/2 tablespoons white wine vinegar

1-1/2 tablespoons lemon juice

2 teaspoons shallots, finely minced

1/4 teaspoon salt

Freshly ground white pepper

1 tablespoon butter for the reduction, plus 4 ounces
chilled unsalted butter, cut into 8 pieces

Combine the vinegar, lemon juice, shallots, salt, pepper and 1 tablespoon butter in a small, heavy, non-reactive saucepan and boil over medium-high heat until reduced to about 1 tablespoon.

Remove the saucepan from the heat and whisk in a few pieces of the chilled butter until they melt creamily into the reduction. Return the saucepan to the burner, and over very low heat add the remaining pieces of butter, one piece at a time, whisking constantly. The sauce should be creamy and pale. Season with salt, pepper and lemon juice as needed. Hold the sauce in a warm spot.

To assemble:

Sauté the scallops in butter for about 2 minutes on each side. Remove from heat and cover for a minute so that scallops are warmed through. On four warmed plates, ladle a tablespoon of Beurre Blanc, swirling to coat the surface. Remove the toothpicks from the scallops and place 3 scallops in the center of each plate. Scatter the lemon zest, chopped chives and caviar around the scallops and serve immediately.

Pork Tenderloin Roasted with Curry Spices, Peach and Ginger Chutney

Serves 4

Ingredients

2 pork tenderloins, about 1 pound each

Salt and pepper

1 tablespoon curry paste, either purchased or made
from your favorite blend of curry spices with
enough vegetable oil added to make a paste

1 cup Peach and Ginger Chutney (recipe follows)

Trim the tenderloins of excess fat and connective
tissue and rub with salt and pepper. Rub with curry
paste and set aside to marinate at room temperature
for about an hour. Meanwhile, make Peach and
Ginger Chutney.

Peach and Ginger Chutney

6 ripe peaches (about 2 pounds)

1/2 cup apple cider vinegar

1 cup brown sugar, packed

1 small lemon, sliced thin and seeded

2 tablespoons peeled and finely diced fresh ginger

2 cloves garlic, minced

1/2 red bell pepper, chopped fine

1 small jalapeño pepper, seeded and minced

1/2 cup golden raisins

1/2 cup raisins

1/2 teaspoon salt

Dip peaches in a pot of boiling water for 1 minute, then
plunge in cold water and slip skins off. Pit peaches and
cut in 1/2-inch dice.

Bring vinegar and sugar to boil in a large, non-corrosive
saucepan. Add the peaches and all of the other
ingredients and bring to a simmer. Cook, stirring
occasionally, until mixture thickens. (Any leftover
chutney can be stored in the refrigerator for several
months and can be used as a condiment for other curries,
as a wonderful relish for ham or turkey sandwiches, or
whisked into a vinaigrette for spinach salad.)

Preheat the oven to 375 degrees.

Blot the tenderloins with paper towels. Heat vegetable
oil in an oven-proof skillet, add the tenderloins and
brown quickly on all sides. Put skillet on a rack in the
center of the oven and roast to an internal temperature
of 150 degrees, 12 to 15 minutes. Remove tenderloins
to a cutting board and let rest for about 5 minutes,
covered loosely with foil. Carve into slices about
1/4 inch thick and divide among 4 dinner plates.
Spoon the chutney decoratively over the pork.
Serve with steamed basmati rice and sautéed spinach.

CHICKEN McKENZIE:
CHICKEN CUTLETS WITH HAZELNUT CRUST AND
PINOT GRIS-THYME CREAM SAUCE

Serves 4

My dear friend and colleague Amedee Smith and I developed this recipe to honor the hazelnut growers of Oregon's McKenzie River Valley.

INGREDIENTS

1 cup Pinot Gris

1 tablespoon finely chopped shallots

2 cups heavy cream

1 tablespoon Dijon mustard

Salt and freshly ground pepper to taste

1 tablespoon finely chopped fresh thyme leaves

1 tablespoon finely chopped parsley

1/2 cup lightly toasted and finely chopped hazelnuts

1/2 cup fresh bread crumbs

1/2 cup flour

1 egg, lightly beaten

4 boneless, skinless chicken breasts

3 tablespoons unsalted butter

In a small saucepan, combine wine and shallots and reduce to 1/4 cup. Add cream, whisk in mustard, and reduce until thick enough to coat a spoon. Add salt and pepper to taste, add the thyme and set aside in a warm place.

Place the chicken breasts between two sheets of waxed paper or parchment paper and, using a rolling pin or cleaver, flatten to an even thickness of about 1/2 inch. Combine chopped hazelnuts and bread crumbs and spread on a baking sheet. Dredge each chicken breast in the flour, shaking off excess. Dip in egg mixture and then in hazelnut mixture to coat evenly.

Melt butter in a sauté pan large enough to hold all the chicken breasts in one layer. Sauté chicken breasts over medium heat until golden brown, turning once. This will take 2 to 3 minutes per side—be careful not to overcook. Drain on paper towels. Meanwhile, bring the sauce back up to temperature and whisk in the chopped parsley. Spoon sauce over each cutlet and serve immediately.

This dish makes great comfort food for a fall evening, accompanied by roasted butternut squash, steamed and buttered mustard greens and a glass of Pinot Gris.

INDEX

ACKNOWLEDGMENTS

The realization of the New American Cuisine Cookbook
was graced by the talent and enthusiasm of many.
We would like to extend special thanks to:

Ed and Carolyn King for their vision
and commitment to our King Estate mission.

All of the participating chefs
for sharing their abundant creativity with us.

Sarah Kemp for lending her considerable charm
and intelligence to the project.

John Rizzo whose luminous photographs give the book color and polish.

Food stylist Carol Ladd for shaping the evocative recipe still lifes.

Funk & Associates Marketing Communications,
especially Beverly Soasey for her artist's eye and
Marcia Schoelen for keeping the project moving forward.

Phil Kimmel and Terry Ross for their astute work with the blue pencil.

Julia Potter and Sulwyn Sparks whose cheerful
assistance in the kitchen was invaluable.

Jeanne Palzinski, our master gardener, for the beautiful bounty
she grows and the inspiration it provides.

The entire King Estate staff for lending their critical palates,
above all Mike Lambert, Brad Biehl, Will Bucklin,
Lauren Feltman and Michael Silacci.

New American Cuisine gratefully acknowledges the support
of their in-kind contributors: All-Clad and Valley River Inn.

1-800-All-Clad
(255-2523)

Close by. But still a million miles away.
1-800-543-8266

King Estate, located southwest of Eugene, Oregon, represents an unparalleled commitment to producing wines of truly exceptional quality. The beautiful 550-acre estate resplendent with magnificent vineyards, a grapevine grafting and propagation facility, nursery, orchards, and a lush organic garden, is crowned by a majestic state of the art winery constructed in the style of a grand European chateau.

Wine production at King Estate focuses on three main varieties, Pinot Noir, Pinot Gris, and Chardonnay, and features the small lot, hands-on winemaking techniques essential to produce the finest wines. King Estate's mission is to produce varietal wines of consistently exceptional quality through meticulous fruit selection and impeccable winemaking practices.